THE CLANDESTINE CAKE CLUB

A YEAR *of* CAKE

100
CELEBRATORY
RECIPES

THE CLANDESTINE CAKE CLUB

A YEAR of CAKE

100 CELEBRATORY RECIPES

LYNN HILL

Quercus

This book is dedicated to all Clandestine Cake Club organisers, past and present, who have helped me bring people together to celebrate and share their love of cake.

CONTENTS

INTRODUCTION

In December 2010, inspired by the popularity of secret supper clubs, I thought it would be fun to create a cake club. The idea was to bring people together over cake, encouraging them to share their love of baking and make new friends in the process. Since the start, the club has had just one rule: attendees must bring a whole cake large enough to share with fellow bakers and guests. Cupcakes, muffins or brownies are not permitted; interaction and conversation begin as you cut the first slice.

From the 11 people and 6 cakes at that very first event, the Clandestine Cake Club (CCC) has grown larger than I ever dreamed was possible – it now has over 14,000 members and nearly 200 clubs dotted all around the UK, as well as several clubs overseas. Bakers and cake lovers gather in secret places – venues are revealed just a few days before the event, and only to those who've booked a place. That's the clandestine part.

Themed events make the occasions more fun and challenging, encouraging bakers to step out of their comfort zone and attempt new flavours and techniques, or get creative with decoration. It's not a competition though, and the cakes aren't judged, they are simply eaten, shared and enjoyed. Any leftovers are distributed among members and taken home for families and co-workers to eat the next day. Such is the butterfly effect of the CCC – everyone gets to eat cake.

The success of the club has resulted in so many exciting opportunities. We've been written about in newspapers, featured in magazines and even appeared on TV, most recently as part of a documentary called *The Icing on the Cake*, presented by Nigel Slater. Nigel and his crew joined us for a very special gathering in Leeds, at which he mingled, chatted and ate cake with CCC members. He even brought his own cake!

In 2013, our first cookbook was published, with recipes contributed by members. To celebrate its launch, we hosted a series of special club events in bookshops up and down the country, sharing the cake love with shoppers and passers-by. Celebration and sharing is at the heart of CCC so now we're back with a second delicious helping – 100 cake recipes that pay homage to some of the most noteworthy events and occasions throughout the year. Many of these are inspired by the numerous Clandestine Cake Club themes that organisers have chosen for their meetings, from international holidays and religious festivals, to charity days, sporting fixtures, famous anniversaries, birthdays of iconic figures, and a whole host of other cake-worthy dates in the diary.

My favourites include the Mona Cake (page 63), a traditional Catalan cake baked at the end of Lent as a way of using up all the eggs that have accumulated over the fasting period. It reminds me of a wonderful trip to visit members based in Barcelona. I also love the Sea Salted Caramel Cake (page 64), included in honour of Nigel Slater's birthday. This is the cake I made when he joined us. And let's not forget the Caramel Pecan Brittle Swiss Roll (page 122), which I devised to mark the anniversary of Bettys Tea Room opening in Harrogate, in July 1919. It's one of my favourite places for afternoon tea.

Besides these delights, in this book you will find an abundance of flavours, ranging from the traditional and much loved, such as vanilla, coffee, chocolate, ginger and citrus, to the more inventive, including saffron, rose hip, masala chai, coconut, cardamom, peanut butter and mango. For adventurous flavour seekers, there are combinations like Bacon and Maple Syrup (page 114), Sweet Potato and Vanilla (page 184), and Spiced Pumpkin (page 169). If you're a fan of Bundt cakes, or in search of gluten-free recipes, we have that covered too.

Our recipes can be a starting point for your own celebration, whatever the event. Whether the cake is for a gathering with friends, a family birthday, a special occasion, or even a wedding, there's something here to inspire you. And that's just the beginning – to make things even more exciting, you could even plan drinks, decorations, music and costumes to fit the theme and complement the cake. So turn up the volume and join me in celebrating a Year of Cake!

Lynn Hill
www.clandestinecakeclub.co.uk

JANUARY

1st January

NEW YEAR'S DAY

GREEK VASILOPITA

6th January

NIGELLA LAWSON'S BIRTHDAY

GUINNESS, CHOCOLATE AND TIA MARIA CAKE

7th January

ORTHODOX CHRISTMAS, BALKANS

REFORM TORTE

8th January

ELVIS PRESLEY'S BIRTHDAY (1935)

PEANUT BUTTER AND CARAMELISED BANANA CAKE

Early to mid January

SEVILLE ORANGE SEASON

ORANGE AND HERB CAKE

25th January

BURNS NIGHT

RASPBERRY CRANACHAN CAKE

26th January

AUSTRALIA DAY

CHERRY LAMINGTON

Flora Loizou

As well as being the start of a new year, in Greece the first day of January is St Basil's Day and it is traditional to serve vasilopita (literally St Basil's bread), a rich cake or bread that is baked with a coin or small trinket inside. It's said that whoever gets the coin will have good luck in the coming year. Flora's moist citrus sponge is beautifully light so who's to stop you having an extra slice in search of the lucky coin? Happy new year!

GREEK VASILOPITA

SERVES 12–14

sunflower oil, for greasing

225g unsalted butter or Stork, softened

450g caster sugar

4 medium eggs

350g plain flour, sifted
(or 230g plain flour
and 120g ground almonds)

1 tbsp baking powder

grated zest and juice of 2 large oranges (you need 250ml of juice so top up with shop-bought orange juice if necessary)

25g flaked almonds

1. Preheat the oven to 180°C/fan 160°C/gas 4. Grease a 28cm cake tin with sunflower oil.

2. Beat the butter and sugar using a wooden spoon or electric whisk, until light and fluffy. Add the eggs one at a time, beating well after each addition, and adding a tablespoon of flour with the final egg to help prevent curdling. Beat in the baking powder and remaining flour until combined, then stir in the orange zest and juice.

3. Pour the mixture into the tin and scatter over the flaked almonds. Bake in the centre of the oven for 50 minutes or until a skewer inserted into the centre of the cake comes out clean. The cake will rise quite dramatically then sink a bit but don't worry, it is just because of the juice.

Joanne Robinson

Domestic goddess Nigella Lawson has several iconic cake recipes to her name, which are often lovingly recreated by Cake Club members for our events. In Joanne's affectionate tribute to Nigella's Chocolate Guinness Cake, not only are the roasted flavours of Guinness beautifully balanced by the smooth, sweet taste of chocolate, but she has upped the temptation factor by adding rum and coffee undertones. It's a pretty seductive cake – perfect for toasting the birthday of this very special British baker.

GUINNESS, CHOCOLATE AND TIA MARIA CAKE

SERVES 8–10

160ml Guinness

160g unsalted butter

4 tbsp Tia Maria (or other coffee-flavoured liqueur), plus extra for brushing

260g caster sugar

2 medium eggs

½ tsp vanilla extract

90ml buttermilk

185g plain flour

50g cocoa powder

1½ tsp bicarbonate of soda

¼ tsp baking powder

icing sugar, to dust (optional)

CHOCOLATE GANACHE

125ml double cream

225g dark chocolate (minimum 50 per cent cocoa solids), roughly chopped

2 tbsp Tia Maria (or other coffee-flavoured liqueur), or to taste

1. Preheat the oven to 190°C/fan 170°C/gas 5. Grease and line two 20cm sandwich tins.

2. Place the Guinness and butter in a saucepan and heat gently. When the butter has melted add the Tia Maria. Take the pan off the heat and stir in the sugar.

3. In a jug, mix together the eggs, vanilla extract and buttermilk. Add to the saucepan.

4. Sift the dry ingredients together into the bowl of an electric mixer or a large bowl, add the wet mixture, and mix on a low speed using the paddle attachment or a hand-held whisk. Make sure all the ingredients are incorporated (but don't mix for longer than 2 minutes) before pouring the mixture into the prepared tins.

5. Bake for 25 minutes or until a skewer inserted in the centre of the cakes comes out clean.

6. While the cakes are in the oven, make the ganache. Heat the cream gently but do not allow to boil. Take off the heat. Stir the chopped chocolate into the cream until completely melted, then stir in the Tia Maria. Leave the ganache to cool and set slightly.

7. Remove the cakes from the oven and while they are still warm brush them with some Tia Maria. Leave for 15 minutes, then brush again with more Tia Maria and leave for a further 15 minutes before turning out on to a wire rack to cool completely.

8. Once the cake is cool, spread about a third of the ganache between the layers of sponge then use the remainder to cover the whole cake. Decorate with a dusting of icing sugar, if you wish.

While in the Western world we base our year around the Gregorian calendar, some Orthodox churches still follow the Julian calendar in which dates fall 13 days later. Consequently many households across the Balkans celebrate Christmas Day in January. After a traditional festive lunch, families gather to enjoy a slice of this rich multi-layered nutty chocolate torte, served with a glass of dessert wine. The history of the cake's name is unknown. Some people say that it has a unique flavour – a reformed taste, shall we say; others that it takes reforms to make such a grandiose cake! Either way, it's one to enjoy with gusto.

Jelena Culum

REFORM TORTE

SERVES 8

10 medium egg whites
(use the yolks in the filling)

8 tbsp caster sugar

pinch of salt

250g ground walnuts or hazelnuts
(both are delicious)

CHOCOLATE FILLING

10 medium egg yolks

8 tbsp caster sugar

200g good-quality dark chocolate
(minimum 70 per cent cocoa
solids), broken into pieces

250g unsalted butter, softened

GLAZE

80g unsalted butter

100g good-quality dark chocolate
(minimum 70 per cent cocoa
solids), broken into pieces

1. Preheat the oven to 180°C/fan 160°C/gas 4. Grease and line four 20cm sandwich tins. If you don't have four tins you can bake the layers free-form by drawing four 20cm circles on to baking parchment and use the paper to line baking trays.

2. In a large bowl, whisk the egg whites with an electric whisk. Slowly add the sugar and mix at a higher speed, adding the salt, until stiff peaks forms.

3. Carefully fold in the ground nuts. Divide the batter between the tins or carefully spoon into the circles on the baking parchment. Bake for 20–25 minutes, until golden brown. Leave in the tins for 5–10 minutes, then turn the cakes out on to a wire rack to cool.

4. For the filling, place the egg yolks, sugar and chocolate in a heatproof bowl set over a pan of simmering water. Stir every minute or so until the mixture is quite thick, then remove from the heat and leave to cool.

5. In a separate bowl, beat the butter until creamy. Once the chocolate mixture is cool, mix it into the butter until well combined.

6. Place one layer of sponge on a serving plate and cover it with a layer of filling about 1cm thick. Repeat until all four layers are stacked on top of each other, then cover the top and sides of the torte with the remaining filling. Place the cake in the fridge for 1 hour to allow the layers to set.

7. To make the glaze, gently heat the butter in a pan. Once melted, remove from the heat and add the chocolate. Mix with a wooden spoon then leave to cool for 5–10 minutes (it needs to be cool enough so as not to melt the butter in the filling below it). Pour the glaze over the whole torte, then leave to set at room temperature. After a few hours (once the glaze is set), you can transfer the cake to the fridge, but you need to take it out at least 2 hours before serving.

Peggy Roegiers

Seville oranges are naturally bitter in taste, so unlike their sweeter cousins, they tend to be used mostly in cooking, such as in pickles, marinades and tangy dressings. They also make some of the best marmalade. They have a famously short season: just a few weeks of voluptuous ripeness in early to mid January. So, if you fancy celebrating their wonderful flavour with this unusual and fragrant recipe, get in there quick while they're in the shops. You'll need to set aside an hour or so for the first stage, which involves boiling the oranges, or do it in advance. It's a clever little trick that brings out the best flavour from these sought-after Spanish treasures and leaves no part unused.

ORANGE AND HERB CAKE

SERVES 12

2 Seville oranges (if you can buy them, or medium-sized regular oranges)

a handful of a mixture of fresh basil, rosemary, thyme and mint leaves

300g plain flour

300g granulated sugar

2 tsp baking powder

1 tsp salt

3 large eggs, at room temperature

175ml olive oil

125ml milk

FILLING

250g mascarpone

2 tbsp soft light brown sugar

about 1 tbsp orange blossom water, to taste

a small handful of a mixture of fresh rosemary, basil, thyme and mint leaves, very finely chopped, to taste

1. Boil the oranges in water for 1 hour. Remove from the pan and let them cool a little, then cut into quarters and remove any pips. Place the oranges and herbs in a food processor and purée until smooth.

2. Preheat the oven to 180°C/fan 160°C/gas 4. Line the base and sides of a 900g loaf tin with baking parchment.

3. In a bowl, mix the flour, sugar, baking powder and salt. Add the eggs, oil and milk and mix with an electric mixer or electric whisk, until everything is blended. Add the orange and herb purée to the mixture and mix again with a spatula. Pour the batter into the tin leaving a 2.5cm gap at the top for the cake to rise and expand (you may have a little more batter than you need).

4. Bake for 1 hour 20 minutes–1½ hours or until a skewer inserted in the centre of the cake comes out clean.

5. Take the cake out of the oven and turn out on to a wire rack to cool completely.

6. To make the filling, mix the mascarpone, sugar and orange blossom water, being careful to add the blossom water slowly and tasting as you go as brands have different strengths. Stir in the herbs, to taste. Slice the cake in half horizontally and spread the filling mix between the layers. Sandwich the layers together and serve.

Lynn Hill
Founder of
Clandestine Cake Club

Burns Night, the birthday of Robert Burns, commemorates the life and work of the much-loved Scottish poet. Celebrations typically involve haggis, whisky and passionate recitations of Burns' poetry, including his famous 'Address to a Haggis'. If you fancy something sweet to follow your haggis, this recipe is the perfect choice. Cranachan is a traditional Scottish dessert, containing raspberries, whipped cream, whisky and honey, topped with toasted oatmeal. Here it's reinvented as a cake, which is just as boozy and creamy as the real thing, not to mention full of Scottish warmth and flavour.

RASPBERRY CRANACHAN CAKE

SERVES 8–10

225g unsalted butter, softened

75g soft light brown sugar

4 large eggs, lightly beaten

300g self-raising flour, sifted

75g rolled oats

150ml clear honey

75ml whisky

OAT TOPPING

80ml clear honey

50g rolled oats

25g flaked almonds

25g mixed nuts, chopped, or any of your favourite nuts

1 tbsp whisky

WHISKY CREAM

300ml double cream

2 tbsp whisky

250g fresh raspberries

1. Preheat the oven to 190°C/fan 170°C/gas 5. Grease and line two 18cm loose-bottomed cake tins.

2. Make the oat topping. Line the base of a small baking tray with greaseproof paper and grease the paper.

3. Gently heat the honey in a small saucepan. Remove from the heat and add the oats and all the nuts, stirring to ensure they are completely coated in the honey. Add the whisky and mix well.

4. Spread the mixture over the baking tray and bake for 14 minutes, stirring halfway to make sure it's not sticking, until slightly crisp and golden. Leave to one side.

5. Beat the butter and sugar using a wooden spoon or electric whisk, until light and fluffy. Add the eggs one at a time, beating well after each addition, and adding a tablespoon of flour with the final egg to help prevent curdling. Add the remaining flour, oats, honey and whisky and mix until well combined. Divide the mixture between the tins.

6. Bake for 25–30 minutes or until a skewer inserted into the centre of each cake comes out clean. Leave in the tins to cool completely before turning out.

7. Make the whisky cream. Whip the cream until it forms soft peaks, being careful not to overbeat. Add the whisky and mix until combined.

8. To assemble, place one of the cake layers on to a serving plate or stand. If the cakes have domed a little you might want to level the tops by slicing off a thin layer so the filling and topping will sit flat. Cover the bottom layer with about half of the whisky cream and a third of the raspberries. Top with the second cake and spread the remaining cream over it. Scatter over the oat topping along with the remaining raspberries and serve. This cake will keep for a few days in the fridge.

Australia Day marks the date when the first fleet of British ships arrived in New South Wales in 1788. Celebrate with the Australians by baking a variation of their national treasure, the lamington cake. This quintessential treat came about thanks to a happy accident. In 1900, the chef to the Governor of Queensland, Lord Lamington, was trying to come up with new and interesting ways to entertain Lamington's guests at afternoon tea and decided to dip some leftover sponge cake in chocolate. Fortunately, the lord and his guests were impressed with the chef's experiment and a cake icon was born. To this day, lamingtons are traditionally made as small square sponges dipped in chocolate then rolled in desiccated coconut. Cake Club rules forbid anything that's not a full cake, so Louise's twist on the classic recipe is a large lamington, filled with a juicy cherry conserve. Why have just a small square when you can get stuck in to a hefty wodge?

Louise Miles-Crust

CHERRY LAMINGTON

SERVES 10–12

260g plain flour

2 tsp baking powder

¼ tsp salt

110g unsalted butter, softened

150g caster sugar

2 large eggs, beaten

1 tsp vanilla extract

grated zest of 1 unwaxed lemon

120ml milk

> *Ingredients and recipe continue overleaf*

1. Preheat the oven to 180°C/fan 160°C/gas 4. Grease a 20cm square cake tin.

2. Sift the flour, baking powder and salt into a large bowl.

3. In a separate bowl, beat the butter and sugar using an electric mixer or whisk, until light and fluffy. Gradually add the beaten eggs, a little at a time, beating well after each addition. Add the vanilla extract and lemon zest and beat until combined. With the mixer on a low speed, alternately add the flour mixture and milk. Start with half the flour, then add the milk and then finish with the remaining flour.

4. Pour the cake batter into the prepared tin and smooth the top with a spatula. Bake for 30–35 minutes or until a skewer inserted in the centre of the cake comes out clean. It is quite a pale sponge so don't be alarmed if the skewer comes out clean but the cake isn't brown.

5. Leave the cake to cool in its tin on a wire rack for 10 minutes, then remove from the tin and leave to cool completely on the wire rack. >

FILLING AND COATING

160g cherry conserve

450g icing sugar, sifted

30g unsweetened cocoa powder

3 tbsp unsalted butter

120ml milk

about 100g unsweetened desiccated coconut

glacé cherries, to decorate

6. To fill and decorate, slice the cake in half horizontally. Spread the conserve evenly over one cake half, then place the other half on top. Put the cake in the fridge for several hours or overnight.

7. For the chocolate coating, sift the icing sugar and cocoa powder into a heatproof bowl and add the butter and milk. Place the bowl over a saucepan of simmering water, making sure the bottom of the bowl does not touch the water. Stir the mixture for 3 minutes, until it becomes smooth. Remove the bowl from the heat and leave the icing to start to set for a few minutes, until it thickens enough to coat the back of a spoon. If you've left it for too long just stir it with a whisk to loosen it again.

8. Take the cake out the fridge and place it on a wire rack that is placed over a baking sheet (to catch the drips). Pour the chocolate mixture over the cake, taking time to make sure it is all covered.

9. Once the cake is covered, sprinkle over the desiccated coconut. The combination of the chocolate and coconut can make this part a bit messy as you have to throw the coconut at the sides of the cake so do this on a surface that can be cleaned easily. Decorate with glacé cherries. Once the cake is set, you can store it in an airtight container for a few days.

Elvis Presley is perhaps the best-loved and most influential rock 'n' roll and pop singer of all time and many ardent fans still celebrate the King's birthday as a way of honouring his life and work. This indulgent birthday cake takes its inspiration from Elvis's favourite sandwich, which famously consisted of peanut butter and banana (his mom fried the bananas in bacon fat for him!). With its delicious peanutty sponge, creamy frosting and crunchy caramelised banana topping, it is guaranteed to be always on your mind.

Yin Li

PEANUT BUTTER AND CARAMELISED BANANA CAKE

SERVES 8–12

200g unsalted butter, at room temperature

3 tbsp peanut butter (crunchy or smooth depending on your preference)

200g golden caster sugar

4 large eggs, preferably at room temperature

150g natural yoghurt

200g self-raising flour

PEANUT BUTTER FROSTING

80g unsalted butter, at room temperature

250g peanut butter (crunchy or smooth)

150g icing sugar, sifted

a few tbsp cream or milk, if required

TOPPING

3 large, under-ripe bananas, cut into 1cm-thick slices

3 tbsp golden caster sugar

1. Preheat the oven to 180°C/fan 160°C/gas 4. Grease and line the base of two 20cm sandwich tins.

2. Beat the butter, peanut butter and sugar using an electric whisk, until fluffy and well combined. Add the eggs and yoghurt to the bowl with a tablespoon of flour to help prevent curdling, and beat again until smooth and creamy.

3. Fold in the remaining flour until combined, then divide the mixture evenly between the tins and level it (the mixture can dome, so leaving a small dip in the middle of the tin can help prevent this).

4. Bake for 25–30 minutes, until risen and golden and a skewer inserted in the centre of the cake comes out clean. Leave to cool completely in the tins, but ensure the sides of the cake are clear of the tins first by running the blunt edge of a knife around them.

5. Once the cake is cool, make the peanut butter frosting. Beat together the butter and peanut butter until well combined, then start to beat in the icing sugar. The icing may be quite thick (depending on the type of peanut butter used) so feel free to add some milk or cream to slacken it – you want a nice spreading consistency that is not too runny or it will fall off the cake.

6. To assemble, peel the paper off the cakes and level the bottom one if needs be so that it is completely flat (the trimmings are the cook's treat or quality-control test). Spread the bottom layer with about half the peanut butter frosting, then top with the second cake. Use the rest of the frosting to cover the top of the cake.

7. To finish, arrange the sliced bananas over the frosting, sprinkle with the sugar and either use a blowtorch to carefully glaze the cake or put the cake under a smoking hot grill until the sugar bubbles and turns golden.

FEBRUARY

4th February
FIRST DISNEY FILM
RELEASED (1938)

PRINCESS TORTA

7th February
CHARLES DICKENS'S
BIRTHDAY (1812)

COCONUT WEDDING CAKE

14th February
VALENTINE'S DAY

RASPBERRY AND LEMON
LOVE HEARTS CAKE

Early to mid February
CARNEVALE

TRICOLORE CAKE

Early to mid February
MARDI GRAS

COFFEE BEAN CAKE

Early to mid February
SHROVE TUESDAY

LEMON PANCAKE CAKE

Mid February
CHINESE NEW YEAR

PERSIMMON, YOGHURT
AND PECAN CAKE

Mid to end February
OSCARS NIGHT

CHOCOLATE AND SALTED
CARAMEL POPCORN CAKE

Late February
YORKSHIRE RHUBARB
FESTIVAL

RHUBARB AND CUSTARD
CRUMBLE CAKE

Lynn Hill
Founder of
Clandestine Cake Club

Snow White and the Seven Dwarfs, Walt Disney's first ever animated feature film, went on national release in February 1938, at which moment the first in an illustrious line of Disney princesses was born. This pretty pastel-coloured cake is a fitting celebration of the 'fairest in the land'. Snowy white whipped cream and a luxurious crème patissière are sandwiched between sponge and engulfed in marzipan – never mind a handsome prince, a slice of this cake is sure to break the spell of any wicked witch.

PRINCESS TORTA

SERVES 12

230g unsalted butter, softened

230g vanilla-flavoured caster sugar or caster sugar mixed with the scraped seeds of 1 vanilla pod

4 medium eggs, lightly beaten

230g self-raising flour, sifted

CRÈME PATISSIÈRE

200ml double cream or whole milk

1 vanilla pod, seeds scraped

60g caster sugar

2 large eggs

30g plain flour

60g unsalted butter

1. Start by making the crème patissière. Pour the cream into a pan and add the vanilla pod and seeds. Scald the milk by placing it over a low heat and bringing it to just below boiling point, then remove from the heat.

2. In a large bowl, whisk together the sugar, eggs and flour until well combined. Gradually pour the milk mixture through a sieve over the egg mixture and mix well, then return to the pan. Place over a low heat and cook gently, whisking constantly to avoid lumps forming; the mixture will soon begin to thicken. Once thick enough to coat the back of a spoon, add the butter and keep mixing until it has melted. Transfer the crème patissière to a bowl and cover the surface with cling film to avoid a skin forming, then leave in the fridge to cool and set. The crème can be kept for up to a few days if required.

3. Preheat the oven to 210°C/fan 190°C/gas 6½. Grease and line the base of two 20cm loose-bottomed sandwich tins.

4. Beat the butter and icing sugar together using a wooden spoon or electric whisk, until light and fluffy. Add the eggs one at a time, beating well after each addition, and adding a tablespoon of flour with the final egg to help prevent curdling. Fold in the remaining flour and mix until well combined.

5. Pour the mixture into the tins, adding a little more to one of them as you will slice this cake in half later to make two layers. Bake in the oven for 20–25 minutes or until a skewer inserted in the centre of the cakes comes out clean. The tin with the extra batter will take around 5 minutes longer. Leave in the tins for 10 minutes to cool, then turn out on to a wire rack to cool completely.

FILLING AND TOPPING

400ml double or whipping cream

50g ready-made raspberry preserve or jam

400g ready-made white marzipan

pink gel food colouring

green gel food colouring

icing sugar, to dust

6. Whip the cream until it is firm and holds its shape. Slice the larger of the cakes in half horizontally. Cover the thickest layer with a thin layer of about half the preserve then a third of the whipped cream, making sure you do not go over the edges. Place the second sponge layer on top and spread this with the remaining preserve and then a layer of crème patissière. Place another third of the whipped cream on top in the centre to form a dome shape. Place the final sponge on top and gently press down taking care to keep the dome shape of the cake. Cover the whole cake in a thin coating of the remaining whipped cream, which will help the marzipan stick. Leave in the fridge to set while you prepare the marzipan covering.

7. Knead the marzipan until pliable, then take off a section about the size of a golf ball. Add a drop or so of pink colouring to the smaller amount and knead again until you have an even colour. Set aside for decoration.

8. Add a few drops of green colouring to the remaining marzipan and knead until well combined, adding more colouring until you reach your desired shade of green. Dust a work surface and rolling pin very lightly with icing sugar and roll out the marzipan until large enough to cover the whole cake (make sure you keep the marzipan moving so that it doesn't dry out and don't use too much icing sugar). Remove the cake from the fridge and carefully cover with the green marzipan, gently smoothing down all the creases. Cut off any excess marzipan at the base of the cake.

9. Cut a flower or any other shape you prefer from the pink marzipan and place on top of the cake. If necessary use some cooled boiled water to help it stick. This cake can be kept in the fridge for up to 3 days.

Deborah Manger

One of the greatest English novelists of the Victorian era, Charles Dickens created some of literature's most colourful characters. *Great Expectations'* Miss Havisham is one of his most memorable. The eccentric spinster lives in perpetual mourning after being jilted on her wedding day and decades later still wears her wedding dress and refuses to leave her crumbling mansion. So how better to mark the birthday of this literary great than with this coconut creation inspired by the wedding that never was. With its coconut flavour and elegant coating, even Miss Havisham would have a hard time not tucking in.

COCONUT WEDDING CAKE

SERVES 10–12

120g coconut oil

8 medium eggs

240g caster sugar

240g plain flour

JAM FILLING

600g mixed berries

500g pectin sugar

juice of 1 lemon

FROSTING

125g unsalted butter, softened

125g mascarpone

500g icing sugar

50g coconut cream

coconut essence, to taste

DECORATION

180g fresh coconut, shredded in a food processor

75g desiccated coconut

You will also need: 4 large drinking straws to support the upper tier

1. Start by making the jam. Mix the fruit, sugar and lemon juice in a pan over a low heat, stirring until the sugar has dissolved. Bring to the boil, then immediately stop stirring, but leave on a gentle rolling boil for 10–15 minutes. Skim off any surface scum then pour the jam into hot sterilised jars and set aside until ready to use.

2. Preheat the oven to 180°C/fan 160°C/gas 4. Grease and line the base and sides of two 20cm cake tins and one deep 10cm cake tin.

3. Melt the coconut oil in a small pan, then leave it to cool.

4. Whisk the eggs and the sugar until pale, light and doubled in volume and the whisk leaves a ribbon trail when lifted out. Very gently fold in half the flour and half the cool coconut oil, then fold in the remaining flour and oil.

5. Divide the cake mixture between the tins, then bake for 25 minutes, until golden and firm to the touch. Turn the cakes out of their tins and once cool enough to handle, peel off the baking parchment and transfer to wire racks to cool completely.

6. For the frosting, beat the butter and mascarpone until light and fluffy. Add the remaining ingredients and beat until smooth. Chill until needed.

7. To assemble the cake, slice the deeper of the 20cm cakes (inevitably cakes rise at different rates so one will be slightly deeper) into two layers and the 10cm cake into three layers. Pipe a ring of frosting around the top edges of the layers that will be topped with jam; this prevents the jam from dripping over the sides of the cake and mixing with the frosting when you cover the whole cake. Assemble the three 20cm layers and the three 10cm layers. Using a palette knife, cover the sides of the cakes with a very thin layer of frosting – a 'crumb coat', then chill for 20–30 minutes.

8. Cover the sides and the tops of the cakes with a full coat of frosting, and carefully sprinkle over a mixture of the fresh and desiccated coconut. Insert the four straws into the centre of the larger cake to create a support for the 10cm cake, and then stick it on top.

Mike Wallis

While we are busy making pancakes in Britain, the Italians throw a huge party in honour of 'carnevale', their final knees-up before the abstinence of Lent. There's music and mischief, dancing and disguises, feasting and fun. Why not host your own carnevale party and serve this colourful cake, inspired by the Italian flag? For authenticity, remember to arrange the sponges in the right order: green (pistachio), white (vanilla), then red (raspberry). The flavours are guaranteed to be remembered long after the music stops.

TRICOLORE CAKE

SERVES 8

180g unsalted butter, softened

180g caster sugar

3 large eggs

180g self-raising flour

½ tsp baking powder

1 tsp vanilla bean paste

1 tbsp raspberry jam, sieved, plus 2 heaped tbsp

red gel food colouring

1 tbsp pistachio paste

green gel food colouring

250g mascarpone

250g white marzipan

icing sugar, to dust

1 tbsp caster sugar

1. Preheat the oven to 180°C/fan 160°C/gas 4. Grease and line three identical 900g loaf tins (or bake each layer separately and use the same tin each time).

2. Beat the butter and sugar using a wooden spoon or electric mixer until light and fluffy. Add the eggs one at a time, beating well after each addition, and adding a tablespoon of flour to prevent curdling. Fold in the remaining flour and the baking powder a third at a time, until just combined.

3. Divide the mixture into 3 equal parts (each weighing about 240g give or take 10g) in separate bowls. Into one bowl gently fold the vanilla bean paste. Into the next add the sieved jam. Put the tip of a teaspoon into the red gel colour and add that to the mix with the jam. Into the third bowl add the pistachio paste and a teaspoon tip of green gel.

4. Pour each into a separate loaf tin and bake for 30 minutes, or until a skewer inserted in the centre of the cakes comes out clean. Don't open the oven for at least the first 20 minutes of cooking. When ready, leave in the tins for a few minutes to cool then turn out on to a wire rack to cool completely.

5. When the cakes are cool, mix together the mascarpone and unsieved jam, then slice the browned tops and bottoms off each cake (leave the sides for now). Sandwich the layers together using half the mascarpone, putting the pistachio layer on the bottom, then the vanilla layer and the raspberry layer on top. Now carefully trim the browned sides of the cakes.

6. Dust a work surface and rolling pin very lightly with icing sugar then roll out the marzipan into a rectangle as long as the cake tin, and four times as wide, keeping it moving and working quickly so it doesn't dry out. Spread with the remaining mascarpone mixture, leaving a gap at each short end, and then wrap the long sides of the cake in the marzipan. Trim the edges and ends of the marzipan so that you have a neat rectangle and the seam is sitting on the side of the cake (if the layers are lined up horizontally), then score the marzipan and roll in the caster sugar. To display, turn the cake on its side (with the seam underneath) so that it resembles the Italian flag: three vertical stripes in green, white and red.

The international version of Shrove Tuesday, Mardi Gras is based on the tradition of having as much fun and good food as possible before the fasting of Lent begins. In many places, it has developed into a whole period of celebration, rather than just one day, with colourful parties, larger-than-life characters and lots of bling. One of the biggest Mardi Gras festivals takes place in New Orleans, where they typically serve up sugary cakes iced in lurid colours and containing a lucky bean or trinket. Taking inspiration from that lucky bean, here's a cake that's a little less garish but most definitely full of beans, with a punchy coffee flavour that will dance on your taste buds. If you are so inclined, add a coffee bean to the cake batter, bringing good luck to the person who finds it (as long as you give out a warning to your guests first, else they might end up with an unexpected dental bill!).

Lynn Hill
Founder of
Clandestine Cake Club

COFFEE BEAN CAKE

SERVES 10–12

1 level tsp fresh coffee granules or fine instant coffee powder

230g unsalted butter, softened

230g dark or light muscovado sugar

3 large eggs, beaten

230g self-raising flour

100ml buttermilk

30g mixed nuts, chopped

FROSTING AND TOPPING

250g mascarpone

2 tbsp icing sugar, sifted

¼ tsp fresh coffee granules or fine instant coffee powder

200ml double cream

20g mixed nuts, chopped

1. Preheat the oven to 210°C/fan 190°C/gas 6½. Grease and line the base of two 20cm loose-bottomed cake tins.

2. Grind the fresh coffee to a fine powder using a pestle and mortar (or use the instant coffee powder). Set aside.

3. Cream the butter and sugar using an electric whisk until paler in colour. Add the ground coffee powder and mix until well combined.

4. Add the eggs a little at a time, beating well after each addition, and adding a tablespoon of flour with the final addition to help prevent curdling. Fold in the remaining flour and mix until well combined. Add the buttermilk and nuts. Mix until well combined, but do not over-beat.

5. Pour the cake mixture into the tins and bake in the oven for 20–25 minutes, until a skewer inserted in the centre of the cake comes out clean. Remove from the oven and leave to cool in the tins for 10 minutes before turning out on to a wire rack to cool completely.

6. Grind the fresh coffee to a fine powder using a pestle and mortar (or use the instant coffee powder). Mix the mascarpone and icing sugar to loosen the cheese, then add the coffee and cream. Mix until well combined. Once the cakes are cool, sandwich together the two sponge layers using a third of the filling mixture, scattering a few nuts on top of the filling before you add the second layer. Pipe or spread the remaining frosting on top then scatter with the remaining nuts to decorate. Due to the fresh cream, this cake needs to be stored in the fridge and will keep for a couple of days.

Margaret Knox

St Valentine's Day has long been associated with love, ever since the Middle Ages. These days, the shops become a frenzy of pink and red, shelves heaving with hearts, chocolates and flowers. In Europe, a more tasteful tradition is for lovers to give each other keys in a bid to 'unlock their heart'. But Cake Club members know the fastest way to your heart is through your stomach, so it's an occasion for cake! Presented with this pink, zingy-flavoured fruity gift, your Valentine's reaction is sure to echo one of the classic Love Heart messages: 'All Mine'!

RASPBERRY AND LEMON LOVE HEARTS CAKE

SERVES 10–12

250g unsalted butter, softened

250g caster sugar

4 large eggs

250g self-raising flour

grated zest of 2 lemons

150g fresh raspberries

pink gel food colouring

FILLING

150g unsalted butter, softened

150g icing sugar, sifted

lemon curd or seedless raspberry jam

DECORATION

4 tbsp seedless raspberry jam

500g ready-to-roll white sugarpaste

pink gel food colouring

icing sugar, for dusting and sticking

1 x packet Love Hearts sweets

1. Preheat the oven to 180°C/fan 160°C/gas 4. Grease and line two 20cm sandwich tins.

2. Beat the butter and sugar using a wooden spoon or electric mixer until light and fluffy. Add the eggs one at a time, beating well after each addition, and adding a tablespoon of flour with the final egg to prevent curdling. Sift in the remaining flour and beat to combine. Fold in the lemon zest and raspberries, then add a drop or so of the pink food colouring to turn the sponge pink

3. Divide the mixture between the tins and level the tops. Bake for 25–30 minutes or until golden and a skewer inserted in the centre of the cakes comes out clean. Remove from the oven and leave to cool in the tins for 5 minutes, then turn out on to a wire rack and leave to cool completely.

4. For the filling, beat the butter and icing sugar until you have a smooth buttercream. To stop your cake sliding around on the serving plate spread a tiny bit of the buttercream on the plate before assembling the cake.

5. Place one sponge on the plate and spread the buttercream over the centre. Cover with the curd or jam and top with the second sponge.

6. To decorate, gently warm the jam, then brush it over the top and sides of the cake.

7. Colour the sugarpaste with a tiny bit of the food colouring (use a cocktail stick) and knead until the colour is even. Dust your work surface with icing sugar and roll out the sugarpaste until it's large enough to cover the cake. Gently lift over the cake and smooth down, then trim the edges.

8. Make up a small amount of thick glacé icing by mixing icing sugar with a little bit of water. Using a small spoon or a cocktail stick, spread a little bit of icing on to the back of a Love Heart and stick on to the cake. Arrange the Love Hearts on the cake as you wish.

Chocolate fudge frosting, caramel-drenched popcorn and some artistic styling make this cake a guaranteed crowd pleaser, and the perfect way to celebrate one of the most glamorous nights in the film industry's calendar. Your friends won't believe their eyes when they realise your bag of popcorn isn't quite what it seems! The Academy Awards, as the Oscars are officially called, were first presented in 1929 at the Hollywood Roosevelt Hotel and are now watched by millions around the world. So get into your glad rags, pour the champagne and cut a decadent slice as you wait for the immortal words, 'And the winner is...'

Racheal Johnson

CHOCOLATE AND SALTED CARAMEL POPCORN CAKE

SERVES 20

270g plain flour

450g caster sugar

125g good-quality cocoa powder

2 tsp bicarbonate of soda

1½ tsp baking powder

1½ tsp salt

90ml vegetable oil

285ml buttermilk

285ml hot brewed coffee

3 large eggs, lightly beaten

3 tsp vanilla extract

SALTED CARAMEL

75g unsalted butter

50g soft light brown sugar

50g caster sugar

50g golden syrup

125ml double cream

1 tsp Maldon salt

❯ *Ingredients and recipe continue overleaf*

1. Preheat the oven to 180°C/fan 160°C/gas 4. Grease and line a 23 x 33 x 5cm traybake tin leaving a 5cm overhang of parchment at each short end to make removing the cake easier.

2. In a large bowl, sift together the dry ingredients then stir with a wooden spoon to combine thoroughly.

3. Beat the wet ingredients in a separate bowl then add to the dry. Mix until just combined (the batter will be very liquidy). Pour into the prepared tin then bake in the middle of the oven for 35–40 minutes or until a skewer inserted in the centre of the cake comes out clean. Leave to cool in the tin for about 10 minutes, then turn out on to a wire rack to cool completely. While the cake is cooling, make the salted caramel and the frosting.

4. For the salted caramel, melt the butter, sugars and syrup in a small, heavy-based saucepan. Let the mixture simmer for 4–5 minutes, swirling the pan occasionally (don't stir), until it darkens to a rich caramel colour. Add the cream (stand back in case it spits) and the salt, swirl again and cook for 1 minute more. Pour the caramel into a clean sterilised jar, then set aside until you're ready to assemble the cake.

5. For the frosting, melt the chocolate by placing it in a glass bowl set over a pan of simmering water – do not let the water touch the bottom of the bowl. Set the melted chocolate aside to cool.

6. Combine the cocoa powder and boiling water in a small bowl and stir to dissolve completely.

7. In a mixing bowl, use an electric hand whisk to beat the butter, icing sugar and salt until pale and fluffy (about 5 minutes). Add the melted chocolate and beat until combined. Finally, beat in the cocoa mixture until fully incorporated. Set aside until you're ready to assemble the cake. ❯

CHOCOLATE FUDGE FROSTING

450g dark chocolate (minimum 70 per cent cocoa solids), broken into pieces

45g good-quality cocoa powder

90ml boiling water

340g unsalted butter, softened

65g icing sugar

pinch of salt

SALTED CARAMEL POPCORN

1 tbsp vegetable oil

50g popping corn

50g unsalted butter

75g soft light brown sugar

2 tbsp golden syrup

1 tsp vanilla extract

½ tsp sea salt

TO DECORATE

1kg ready-to-roll white sugarpaste

500g ready-to-roll red sugarpaste

icing sugar, to dust

8. To assemble, cut the cake in half widthways, and then slice each half horizontally through the middle so that you're left with four layers. Place one layer on a board and spread with a third of the salted caramel. Repeat with a further two layers, then place the final layer on top. Wrap the cake in cling film then chill for 30 minutes to help it keep its shape.

9. Remove the cake from the fridge, and trim if needed to give it sharp edges. Using a palette knife, cover the cake with a very thin layer of frosting – a 'crumb coat'. Chill the cake for a further 30 minutes, before adding a full coat of frosting. Again, smooth with a palette knife, and chill for a final 30 minutes.

10. Lightly dust a work surface and rolling pin with icing sugar, then roll out the white sugarpaste into a large rectangle, roughly the thickness of a pound coin. Take the cake out of the fridge and drape the sugarpaste over it, covering three of the four sides completely and leaving one short side uncovered but with a 2.5cm overhang of icing – this will be the top of your popcorn bag. Use cake smoothers to smooth out the icing, then trim the sugarpaste neatly, leaving the overhang on the open end intact.

11. Roll out the red sugarpaste in the same way. Using a sharp knife or pizza cutter, cut it into 1cm-wide strips. Fill an egg cup with a little water then use your fingertips to dab the strips with a little water one at a time. Arrange each one on the cake, pressing down lightly to stick. Leave a 1cm gap between each strip to create a striped effect, then trim the ends to neaten.

12. Make the popcorn. Line two baking sheets with baking parchment. Heat the oil in a large, heavy-based pan with a tight lid. Add the corn, cover and cook over a medium heat until the popping stops, shaking the pan frequently to stop it from catching. Remove from the heat. Next, melt the butter, sugar, syrup and vanilla in a separate pan. Simmer for 4–5 minutes until the mixture is a rich caramel colour, then stir in the salt. Pour the caramel over the popcorn and stir until it is coated – work quickly. Tip the popcorn on to the trays and spread out in a thin layer. Leave for a couple of minutes, until cool enough to handle but still malleable, then stick it on to the 'open' end of the cake, stuffing it under the sugarpaste to look like it is spilling out of the popcorn 'bag'.

Shrove Tuesday, also known as Pancake Day, is your last opportunity to feast on cake if you plan to observe the 40 days of fasting during Lent, which begins the next day. For cake lovers it is the perfect excuse for indulgence and this innovative no-bake cake is just the ticket for using up all the eggs and flour you are supposed to be foregoing during the next few weeks. Cleverly created using layered-up pancakes, sandwiched with a creamy lemon filling, you're guaranteed to enjoy a deliciously sweet treat. If you like your cakes a little deeper, double the quantities and make twice as many pancakes.

Gillian Tarry

LEMON PANCAKE CAKE

SERVES 8

140g plain flour

2 tsp icing sugar, plus a little extra to serve

2 large or 3 medium eggs, beaten

225ml milk

unsalted butter or vegetable oil, for frying

LEMON CREAM AND FILLING

300ml double cream

zest of 2 lemons and juice of 1

1 x 325g jar of shop-bought lemon curd

1. Line a 23cm loose-bottomed cake tin with cling film (it helps to wet the inside of the tin so that the cling film sticks).

2. Sift the flour and icing sugar into a large bowl, make a well in the centre and add the eggs, then gradually whisk in the milk until you have a smooth batter without any lumps.

3. To cook the pancakes, heat a little butter or oil in a 20cm non-stick frying pan. Add a thin coating of batter and fry over a medium heat until golden on each side. Repeat until all the batter has been used up – you should have about eight pancakes. Stack the pancakes on a plate, interleaved with baking parchment, and leave to cool.

4. To make the lemon cream, beat the cream with the lemon zest and juice until thick and creamy. Do not overbeat.

5. To assemble, place a pancake in the bottom of the tin, spread with lemon curd, then cover with another pancake. Spread the second layer with lemon-flavoured cream, then repeat these layers, alternating the fillings, until a stack is formed, finishing with a pancake on top.

6. Cover the tin with cling film and place in the fridge for several hours or preferably overnight to set. Unwrap the cake when ready to serve and sprinkle with a little icing sugar.

This cake comes courtesy of the club in Wakefield, a town which is one corner of Yorkshire's famous 'Rhubarb Triangle', where Britain's treasured forced rhubarb is grown and harvested in dark forcing sheds lit only by candlelight. Forced rhubarb, which appears much earlier than traditionally grown outdoor rhubarb, is known for its striking bright pink stalks, and Wakefield's annual rhubarb festival is a celebration of its unique sweet and delicate flavour. There have been many rhubarb-themed CCC events in honour of the festival, and the classic pairing of rhubarb and custard is always a big draw; Racheal's recipe proves why. Make the celebration doubly good by using the fruit cooking juices to make rhubarb Bellinis.

Racheal Johnson

RHUBARB AND CUSTARD CRUMBLE CAKE

SERVES 10–12

200g unsalted butter, softened

200g caster sugar

pinch of salt

4 medium eggs, beaten

1 tsp vanilla extract

170g self-raising flour

30g custard powder (not instant)

icing sugar, to dust (optional)

RHUBARB FILLING

400g Yorkshire rhubarb, trimmed

1 tbsp caster sugar

CRÈME PATISSIÈRE

240ml whole milk

½ vanilla pod, split in half

3 medium egg yolks

50g caster sugar

20g cornflour

15g unsalted butter

50ml double cream

> *Ingredients and recipe continue overleaf*

1. Preheat the oven to 200°C/fan 180°C/gas 6. Grease and line two 20cm sandwich tins.

2. For the rhubarb filling, wash but don't dry your rhubarb, then cut it into 2.5cm lengths. Arrange in an ovenproof dish in a single layer, then sprinkle over the sugar. Roast in the oven for 10–15 minutes, until just softened. Remove from the oven, then leave to drain in a sieve set over a bowl – you can reserve the juices to make rhubarb Bellinis. Lower the oven setting to 175°C/fan 155°C/gas 3½.

3. For the crème patissière, pour 160ml of the milk into a heavy-based saucepan. Scrape the seeds from the vanilla pod into the milk, then add the pod and heat the milk over a low heat until almost boiling.

4. In a bowl, whisk the egg yolks and sugar. Mix the cornflour with the remaining milk, then add to the egg and sugar mixture. Remove the vanilla pod from the warm milk, then gradually pour it over the egg mixture, whisking constantly. Clean out the saucepan to remove any milk solids coating it, then pour the mixture back into the clean pan through a sieve. Bring to the boil gently over a medium heat, stirring continuously. Boil for around 1 minute to thicken, whisking as if your life depended on it if the custard starts to split.

5. Once thickened, add the butter and stir until melted. Pour the crème patissière into a medium bowl, then cover the surface of the custard with cling film to prevent a skin forming. Chill immediately until needed. >

CRUMBLE TOPPING

4 tbsp unsalted butter, slightly softened and cut into pieces

75g plain flour

110g granulated sugar

6. Make the crumble topping by rubbing the butter into the flour with your fingertips until it forms pea-sized lumps. Mix in the sugar using a table knife. Set the crumble mix aside.

7. For the cake itself, cream together the butter, sugar and salt in a large bowl using an electric hand whisk, until pale and very fluffy. In a jug, beat the eggs and vanilla extract, then add to the butter and sugar in 4–5 additions, beating well after each one. When all of the egg has been incorporated, sift the flour and custard powder together over the egg and butter mixture, then fold in gently until just combined.

8. Divide the batter equally between the tins and sprinkle the crumble mixture over one tin – this will be the top layer. Bake for 15–20 minutes or until a skewer inserted in the middle of the cake comes out clean. You may find the crumble layer needs a few minutes longer – possibly up to about 10 minutes. Let the cakes cool in the tins for about 10 minutes, then turn out on to a wire rack to cool completely. Be very careful turning out the crumble-covered cake to prevent the crumble sliding off.

9. Just before assembling you will need to loosen the crème patissière to be able to spread it. Push the mixture through a sieve, then stir to bring it together. Whip the double cream until it just starts to thicken and hold its shape, then stir it into the crème patissière. Place the bottom cake layer on a cake plate or board and spread generously with the crème patissière, leaving a 1cm border all the way around to avoid oozing. Spoon the drained rhubarb over the top. Finish with the crumble layer, then dredge with icing sugar, if desired.

The Spring Festival, or Lunar New Year, is the grandest and most important date in the Chinese calendar. Steeped in tradition and superstition, the Chinese hope to encourage the good omens that will bring them an auspicious year. The golden yellow, delicate persimmon fruit (also known as a Sharon fruit) is native to China and a popular offering around this time as it is thought to symbolise luck and sweetness – anything considered 'golden' is believed to bring good fortune. So why not celebrate the Chinese New Year and encourage your own good luck with this cake? Do remember to eat persimmons when they are very soft and ripe or you could find your lips puckering at their sourness. They discolour quickly once cut, so sprinkle a little lemon over the cut sides if you want to conserve their brightness.

Fiona Bevans

PERSIMMON, YOGHURT AND PECAN CAKE

SERVES 10

2 persimmons, peeled
and cut into strips

200g unsalted butter, softened

200g caster sugar

4 medium eggs

200g self-raising flour

1 tsp baking powder

1 tsp ground cinnamon

1 tsp vanilla essence

FILLING AND TOPPING

200g Greek yoghurt

100g icing sugar, sifted

1 tsp vanilla essence

1 persimmon, peeled
and chopped into 3cm cubes

clear honey, to drizzle

whole pecans, to decorate

1. Preheat the oven to 190°C/fan 170°C/gas 5. Grease two 20cm sandwich tins and line with a circle of baking parchment.

2. Put the persimmons into a blender and blitz to a purée.

3. In a large bowl, beat the butter and sugar using a wooden spoon or electric whisk, until light and fluffy. Add the eggs one at a time, beating well after each addition, and adding a tablespoon of flour with the final egg to help prevent curdling. Add the remaining flour, baking powder, cinnamon, vanilla essence and persimmon purée and beat again until combined.

4. Divide the mixture equally between the tins, smoothing the tops with the back of a spoon. Bake for 30 minutes, until golden and the cake springs back when gently pressed. Check that a skewer inserted into the centre comes out clean; if there is a little mixture on the skewer leave the cakes in for a further 3 minutes. Remove from the oven, leave to cool in the tins for about 10 minutes, then turn out and place on a wire rack to cool completely.

5. For the filling, mix the yoghurt, icing sugar and vanilla essence and leave in the fridge.

6. When the cake is completely cool, spread half the yoghurt filling over the bottom cake and place the persimmon pieces on top. Sandwich the two cakes together and top with the remaining filling. Decorate with a drizzle of honey and pecans. Due to the fruit and yoghurt in the cake, it will need to be kept in an airtight container in the fridge to ensure the yoghurt doesn't melt and turn sour. Allow it to come to room temperature to serve.

MARCH

1st March
ST DAVID'S DAY

WELSH HONEY AND
CAMOMILE BARA BRITH

8th March
INTERNATIONAL
WOMEN'S DAY

STRAWBERRY AND
ROSEMARY LOAF

12th March
MRS BEETON'S BIRTHDAY
(1836)

CARAWAY SEED AND APRICOT
BRANDY CAKE

17th March
ST PATRICK'S DAY

IRISH CREAM CAKE

Mid March
RED NOSE DAY

RED BUTTERMILK CAKE

Mid to late March
MOTHER'S DAY

CARDAMOM ROSE CAKE

24th March
MARY BERRY'S
BIRTHDAY (1935)

MIXED BERRY CAKE

29th March
FIRST LONDON
MARATHON (1981)

CHOCOLATE AND PEANUT
FUDGE CAKE

Sam Smith

Bara brith means 'speckled bread' in Welsh and is a delicately spiced fruity tea loaf. It is sometimes made with yeast to make it more like a bread but this version is anchored firmly in the cake category with the use of self-raising flour, which keeps it wonderfully sticky and moist. As a tea bread, soaking the fruit in a brew is obligatory and Sam has chosen to steep hers in a camomile and honey tea, giving it a unique aromatic flavour. It's an easy recipe to bake with children and the perfect cake to celebrate the feast of St David, the patron saint of Wales who died on this day in 569 AD. *Mwynhewch eich bara brith*! (Enjoy your bara brith!)

WELSH HONEY AND CAMOMILE BARA BRITH

SERVES 8–10

275g mixed dried fruit (such as currants, sultanas, raisins, dried apricots, glacé cherries, cranberries)

1 camomile and honey teabag

3 tbsp good-quality clear honey

1 large egg, lightly beaten

85g soft light brown sugar

grated zest of 1 lemon

350g self-raising flour

1 tsp ground mixed spice

butter, to serve (optional)

1. The night before you want to bake the cake you need to soak the dried fruit. Place it in a large mixing bowl. In a measuring jug, make up the camomile and honey tea with 350ml boiling water. Discard the teabag after steeping for about 10 minutes. Stir the honey into the tea and mix well. Pour over the dried fruit and leave to soak overnight, preferably covering it with a tea towel.

2. The next day, preheat your oven to 180°C/fan 160°C/gas 4. Grease and line a 900g loaf tin with baking parchment or use a loaf tin liner (available from most good cookware shops and larger supermarkets).

3. Strain the dried fruit into a large mixing bowl, reserving the liquid. Stir the beaten egg into the fruit.

4. Add the remaining ingredients to the fruit, folding them in carefully to ensure that everything is mixed well. Gradually add the reserved soaking liquid bit by bit until the mixture has a dropping consistency. Pour the mixture into the tin and bake for 1½ hours, until the cake is risen and firm to the touch. If the cake looks as though it is browning too quickly, cover it with foil to allow it to bake for the full time.

5. Leave in the tin to cool for 5–10 minutes, then turn out on to a wire rack to cool completely. Serve with or without butter.

Marked in many countries around the world, and supported by the UN, International Women's Day is a celebration of women's economic, political and social achievements in the pursuit of equality. This cake combines two symbols of femininity. It was once believed that where rosemary grew abundantly outside a house, it was a sign that the household was ruled by a strong woman. As a result, men were known to rip up rosemary bushes in a bid to show that they in fact ruled the roost, not their wives! As for strawberries, these have long been associated with fertility, often depicted in art alongside the Virgin Mary, and in mythology as a symbol of Venus, Goddess of Love, and the Pagan goddess Mother Earth. As you tuck into a slice of this fragrant cake, reflect for a moment on the challenges faced over the years and the sacrifices made to secure the opportunities women enjoy today.

Samantha Ambrose

STRAWBERRY AND ROSEMARY LOAF

SERVES 8–10

200g plain flour

2½ tsp baking powder

100g salted butter, at room temperature

200g golden caster sugar

1 medium egg

100ml semi-skimmed milk

½ tsp vanilla essence

2 tsp finely chopped rosemary

200g strawberries, hulled and chopped into quarters, plus 2 halved strawberries

1 tbsp granulated sugar

1 tsp ground almonds (optional)

small sprig of fresh rosemary, to decorate

1. Preheat the oven to 180°C/fan 160°C/gas 4. Grease and line a 900g loaf tin with baking parchment.

2. Sift the flour and baking powder together into a bowl.

3. In a separate large bowl, beat the butter and sugar together with an electric whisk, until pale and fluffy. Add the egg and milk and beat again until well combined. Lightly beat in the vanilla and rosemary.

4. Fold in half the flour mixture, until combined, then fold in the remaining flour. Gently fold in the quartered strawberries until just combined, then pour the mixture into the prepared tin and gently even out the top.

5. Place the halved strawberries cut-side down in a line down the middle of the loaf then sprinkle the granulated sugar across the top of the loaf, followed by the ground almonds, if you wish.

6. Bake in the centre of the oven for 45–55 minutes, until golden on top and lacking in any movement. Remove from the oven and leave to rest in the tin for 5 minutes before turning out on to a wire rack to cool. Once cool, serve the cake with a sprig of rosemary on the top.

First published in 1861, Isabella Beeton's timeless classic, *Mrs Beeton's Book of Household Management*, is a guide to running a Victorian household. Containing thousands of recipes, it remains a mainstay of cooks and bakers around the world, influencing and inspiring the way we cook today.

In celebration of the birthday of one of the most famous cookery writers of all time, here is an interpretation of a very popular Victorian seed cake from her book. The sponge is light and aromatic with the distinct flavour of the caraway seeds, while a hint of brandy adds a sophisticated, celebratory touch.

Lynn Hill
Founder of
Clandestine Cake Club

CARAWAY SEED AND APRICOT BRANDY CAKE

SERVES 8–10

80g unsalted butter

220g self-raising flour

pinch of salt

pinch of freshly grated nutmeg

4 medium eggs

280g caster sugar

70ml double cream

50ml apricot brandy
or a brandy of your choice

1 tsp caraway seeds

TOPPING (OPTIONAL)

1 tbsp icing sugar

½ tsp freshly grated nutmeg

caraway seeds

1. Preheat the oven to 190°C/fan 170°C/gas 5. Grease an 18cm deep-sided cake tin and line with a cake liner (especially if using a loose-bottomed tin as this batter can be a little runny and you don't want to lose a drop).

2. Melt the butter in a small saucepan and leave to one side to cool.

3. Sift the flour, salt and nutmeg into a bowl and leave to one side.

4. Beat the eggs and sugar together until light and creamy and well combined. Gradually add the cooled melted butter, the cream and brandy and mix together until well combined. Fold in the flour mixture followed by the caraway seeds and give it a good mix so that there are no lumps in the batter. Pour into the cake tin and bake for 50–55 minutes or until a skewer inserted in the centre of the cake comes out clean. Leave the cake in the tin to cool.

5. If making the topping, mix the icing sugar and nutmeg together and dust over the top of the cake when ready to eat. Sprinkle with a few caraway seeds if you wish.

Lynn Hill
Founder of
Clandestine Cake Club

Red Nose Day takes place every two years, organised by British charity Comic Relief to raise money for the poor and disadvantaged in the UK and Africa. In return for donating, you become the proud owner of the eponymous red nose, which gets a makeover each year. Past noses have had arms, hair and stick-on features; they've been glittery, furry and made of foam; one 'hooted' when squeezed and another was designed to look like a tomato. Fundraisers often hold cake sales and this bright red cake would be a perfect contribution. The buttermilk keeps the sponge beautifully moist so expect to sell out as soon as the doors open.

RED BUTTERMILK CAKE

SERVES 8–10

150ml buttermilk

½ tsp high-strength red gel food colouring

175g unsalted butter, softened

225g soft light brown sugar

3 medium eggs

275g self-raising flour, sifted

1 tsp vanilla paste

FROSTING

200g full-fat cream cheese

20g icing sugar, sifted

200g double cream

1 tsp vanilla paste

1. Preheat the oven to 190°C/fan 170°C/gas 5. Grease and line two 20cm loose-bottomed sandwich tins.

2. In a jug, mix the buttermilk and red colouring until well combined; this will help distribute the colour evenly through the cake batter. Leave to one side.

3. Using an electric whisk, beat the butter and sugar until light and fluffy. Add the eggs one at a time, beating well after each addition, and adding a tablespoon of the flour with the final egg to help prevent curdling. Add the vanilla paste, half the buttermilk and half the remaining flour and mix until well incorporated. Add the remaining buttermilk and flour and mix until well combined, making sure that the red colour is evenly distributed through the batter.

4. Divide between the tins and bake in the oven for 20–25 minutes or until a skewer inserted in the centre of the cake comes out clean. Leave in the tins for 10 minutes before turning out on to a wire rack to cool completely.

5. Make the frosting by mixing the cream cheese and icing sugar together until incorporated. This should loosen the cream cheese a little. Add the double cream and vanilla paste and mix until you have a thick spreading consistency. If you think you have overwhipped, just add a little more double cream to bring it back to a manageable thickness.

6. Sandwich the cakes with half the frosting, then spread the remaining half on the top.

Fiona Bevans

Toasting Ireland's patron saint must surely be done with Irish whiskey, while for those of us who like to indulge our sweet tooth, a slice of cake is definitely in order too. Better still, combine them, with this creamy, whiskey-flavoured, tipple-in-a-cake ode to Saint Patrick. Fiona has created her own version of the popular Irish cream liqueur to flavour her sponge and frosting, but you can just use a shop-bought version.

IRISH CREAM CAKE

SERVES 12–14

250g unsalted butter, softened

350g caster sugar

400g plain flour

4 medium eggs

1 tsp baking powder

200ml buttermilk

25g whole almonds, to decorate

IRISH CREAM LIQUEUR
(optional; see introduction)

50g good-quality dark chocolate (minimum 70 per cent cocoa solids), roughly broken

300ml Irish whiskey

100ml double cream

150ml single cream

1 x 400g can condensed milk

1 tsp instant coffee granules

1 tsp almond essence

1 tsp vanilla extract

IRISH BUTTERCREAM

225g icing sugar, sifted

110g unsalted butter

4 tbsp Irish cream liqueur (see recipe above or use a shop-bought version)

1. Preheat the oven to 190°C/fan 170°C/gas 5. Grease and line the base and sides of a deep 23cm cake tin leaving at least 5cm of paper above the rim of the tin to allow the cake to rise.

2. Start to prepare the Irish cream liqueur, if making. Melt the chocolate in a bowl over a pan of simmering water. Set aside to cool for 10 minutes.

3. While you wait for the chocolate to cool, make the cake mixture. Beat the butter and sugar in a large bowl using a wooden spoon or electric whisk until light and fluffy. Add half the flour and 2 of the eggs and beat for 2 minutes. Add the remaining eggs, baking powder, buttermilk and remaining flour and beat for a further 2 minutes.

4. Into a blender put all the remaining ingredients for the Irish cream liqueur and add 2 tablespoons of the melted chocolate. Blend for 45 seconds. Measure out 100ml of this Irish liqueur (or the shop-bought one), add it to the cake mixture and beat together until combined.

5. Pour the mixture into the prepared tin and bake for 1 hour 20 minutes to 1½ hours or until a skewer inserted in the middle of the cake comes out clean. Remove from the oven and leave to cool in the tins for 10 minutes, then turn out on to a wire rack to cool completely.

6. For the buttercream, beat the icing sugar and butter with a wooden spoon for 1 minute and then continue to beat with an electric hand whisk on a low speed. Gradually add the Irish cream liqueur, a tablespoon at a time, until the mixture is smooth and soft enough to spread on the cake. Store any remaining liqueur in a sterilised bottle or large jar, it will keep for up to 4 weeks. Shake before serving.

7. Spread the buttercream all over the top and sides of the cake and decorate with the almonds.

With over 60 years of cookery experience and more than 70 cookbooks to her name, Mary Berry's contribution to British baking is unrivalled. Deservedly considered the queen of cake, she graces our TV screens with boundless energy and enthusiasm, steadfast in her mission 'to get everyone baking'. So what better way to celebrate Mary's birthday than with a fantastic 'berry' cake: bright fresh berries sandwiched with a beautifully light vanilla sponge and lashings of rich clotted cream. So what are you waiting for? 'On your marks, get set... Bake.'

Marie-Anne Crawley

MIXED BERRY CAKE

SERVES 8–10

250g unsalted butter, softened

250g caster sugar

4 large eggs

250g self-raising flour

1 tsp vanilla extract

1–2 tbsp milk

FILLING

2 x 225g tubs clotted cream

225g raspberries

225g tayberries

225g loganberries

1 tbsp icing sugar, sifted

1. Preheat the oven to 180°C/fan 160°C/gas 4. Grease and line the base of two 20cm sandwich tins.

2. Beat the butter and sugar using a wooden spoon or electric whisk, until light and fluffy.

3. Add the eggs one at a time, beating well after each addition, and adding a tablespoon of flour with each egg to prevent curdling. Beat in the vanilla extract, then gradually fold in the remaining flour. Slowly add 1–2 tablespoons of milk until the mixture is loose and creamy.

4. Divide the mixture between the tins and level the tops with a spoon or spatula. Bake for 30–35 minutes, until well risen and golden brown. Allow to cool in the tins for 5–10 minutes before turning out on to a wire rack to cool completely.

5. To assemble, starting at the edges of the top of your base sponge, scoop teaspoons of clotted cream from the tub on to the sponge to create a filling as thick as you like. Try to make sure the cream's crust can be seen on the outer edges of the sponge once assembled as this looks very attractive. Spread a thin layer of the clotted cream (without crust, taken from the centre of the tub) on the bottom side of your upper sponge layer to seal the sponge and stop the berries seeping in. Stand the berries upright on the cream on the bottom layer and sandwich the two sponges together. Dust with the icing sugar.

Nisha Arthey

We shouldn't really need a reason to spoil our mums but Mother's Day does provide the perfect excuse. And what better way to show your mum how much you love her than by making her a cake? This delicate cardamom-spiced sponge, baked in a beautiful Bundt tin then drizzled with a pretty rose-flavoured glaze, is bound to make mums everywhere feel very special indeed.

CARDAMOM ROSE CAKE

SERVES 10–12

cake release spray, for the tin

215g unsalted butter, softened

3 large eggs

1 x 400g can condensed milk

2 tbsp rose water

260g self-raising flour

1 tsp baking powder

1 tsp ground cardamom
(ground seeds from
approximately 20 pods)

100g icing sugar

ROSE WATER SYRUP

100g icing sugar

3 tbsp rose water, or to taste

cardamom pods (optional)

1. Preheat the oven to 180°C/fan 160°C/gas 4. Spray a 25 x 7cm Bundt tin with cake spray.

2. Beat the butter using an electric mixer until creamy.

3. Whisk the eggs and add to the butter along with the condensed milk, rose water, flour, baking powder and cardamom. Mix together until the mixture is evenly combined (be careful not to over mix it).

4. Pour the batter into the prepared tin. Bake in the oven for 30–35 minutes or until a skewer inserted into the cake comes out clean.

5. Towards the end of the baking time, put the icing sugar for the syrup in a pan and add the rose water, being careful to add it slowly and tasting as you go, as brands have different strengths. Add the cardamom pods, if using, and heat gently until the sugar has dissolved.

6. As soon as the cake comes out of the oven, prick it all over with a skewer. Strain the syrup and pour two thirds of it over the cake, in the tin. Leave for 5 minutes or until the syrup has been absorbed then remove the cake from the tin on to a wire rack set over a baking tray. Prick the top of the cake a few times all the way round and pour the remaining syrup over the top (it will drip down the sides but the tray will catch the spills). Leave to cool.

7. To make a glaze, add enough water to the icing sugar to form a runny icing and drizzle over the cooled cake using a spoon or piping bag.

Sharon Clarkson

About 40,000 people pull on their running shoes each year to take part in the challenge that is the London Marathon. Those of us who can't speak from experience can nonetheless imagine that running 26 miles leaves you pretty tired and in need of some energy. With its crunchy, sugar-boosting mix of caramel, peanuts and chocolate, Sharon's 'marathon' cake will definitely help the runners in your life replace the calories they've burned. And if just the thought of running for a bus makes you tired, then sit down with a cup of tea and a slice of cake and toast those brave competitors who pound the streets for charity.

CHOCOLATE AND PEANUT FUDGE CAKE

SERVES 10–12

200g smooth peanut butter

125g icing sugar

225g plain flour

90g cocoa powder

1 tsp salt

1½ tsp bicarbonate of soda

250g unsalted butter, softened

100g caster sugar

330g light brown muscovado sugar

3 large eggs

240ml buttermilk

135ml sour cream

1 tbsp vanilla essence

150g dark chocolate (minimum 70 per cent cocoa solids), chopped

CHOCOLATE FUDGE FROSTING

170g unsalted butter, softened

8 tbsp cocoa powder, sifted

450g icing sugar, sifted

2 tsp vanilla essence

120ml evaporated milk

1. Preheat the oven to 200°C/fan 180°C/gas 6. Grease and line two 23cm cake tins.

2. Mix the peanut butter and icing sugar together until fully combined, then set aside.

3. Sift the flour, cocoa powder and salt together into a bowl.

4. In a separate large bowl, beat the butter and sugars using a wooden spoon or electric whisk, until light and fluffy. Add the eggs one at a time, beating well after each addition. Add a third of the dry ingredients and mix until well combined, then add the buttermilk. Add another third of the dry ingredients. Add the sour cream and vanilla essence and then the remaining dry ingredients until everything is mixed, then gently fold in the chocolate.

5. Place a quarter of the cake batter in each tin then dot teaspoons of the peanut butter mixture over the top. Cover each tin with the remaining batter and bake the cakes for 45–50 minutes or until a skewer inserted in the middle comes out clean. Leave to cool in the tins for 10 minutes, then turn out on to a wire rack to cool completely.

6. While the cakes are in the oven, make the frosting. Whisk the butter with an electric hand whisk until creamy, then beat in the sifted cocoa and icing sugar until combined. Finally beat in the vanilla and evaporated milk.

7. Once cool, sandwich the cakes with half the frosting, then cover the top of the cake with the remainder.

APRIL

Early April

EASTER

CREME EGG NEST CAKE

Early April

EASTER MONDAY

MONA CAKE

9th April

NIGEL SLATER'S
BIRTHDAY

SEA SALTED
CARAMEL CAKE

21st April

BIRTHDAY OF QUEEN
ELIZABETH II (1926)

CAKE FIT FOR A QUEEN

22nd April

EARTH DAY

SAFFRON, ROSE HIP
AND GINGER CAKE

23rd April

WORLD BOOK DAY

PEACH AND CARAMEL
BOOK CAKE

26th April

WILLIAM SHAKESPEARE'S
BIRTHDAY (1564)

STRAWBERRY ROSE
CAKE

For many of us, Easter conjures up images of bunnies, eggs, a lovely long weekend and the chance to indulge our chocolate obsession. But for many others, Easter retains its religious significance as one of the most important days in the Christian calendar, commemorating the death and resurrection of Jesus and symbolising the beginning of new life. Hens' eggs, a forbidden food during the final week of Lent, were traditionally hard-boiled and then decorated to be given as gifts or, as legend tells, distributed by the Easter bunny, then sometimes consumed. Save the real eggs for breakfast and serve up this chocolatey nest for tea. Just make sure there are enough Creme Eggs to go around!

Lynn Hill
Founder of
Clandestine Cake Club

CREME EGG NEST CAKE

SERVES 10–12

cake release spray, for the tin

100g dark chocolate
(minimum 50 per cent
cocoa solids), broken up

250g self-raising flour

½ tsp baking powder

200g unsalted butter, softened

250g golden syrup sugar
(or golden caster sugar
if unavailable)

3 large eggs

1 tsp vanilla paste or vanilla
extract or the scraped seeds
of 1 vanilla pod

150ml buttermilk

> *Ingredients and recipe
continue overleaf*

1. Preheat the oven to 190°C/fan 170°C/gas 5. Spray a 23 x 10cm Bundt tin with cake release spray. (I used the Nordic Ware Chiffon Bundt pan for this cake as it gives a lovely raised nest effect but do use whatever Bundt tin you have; just make sure the dimensions are similar).

2. Melt the chocolate in a bowl set over a pan of simmering water, making sure the bottom of the bowl does not touch the water. Take the bowl off the heat and leave the chocolate to one side to cool but do not let it set.

3. In a separate bowl, sift the flour and baking powder together. Set aside.

4. In a large bowl, beat the butter and sugar using a wooden spoon or electric whisk, until light and fluffy. Add the eggs one at a time, beating well after each addition, and adding a tablespoon of the flour mixture with the final egg to help prevent curdling. Add the remaining flour and mix until well combined. If using a whisk, do this on a low speed so as not to overwork the gluten in the flour.

5. Add the vanilla paste, buttermilk and cooled melted chocolate and mix until well combined (again on a low speed if using a whisk). Pour the batter into the tin and bake in the centre of the oven for 50–55 minutes or until a skewer inserted in the cake comes out clean. Leave to cool in the tin for 10–15 minutes before very carefully turning out on to a wire rack to cool completely. >

GANACHE AND TOPPING

300g dark chocolate (minimum 50 per cent cocoa solids), finely grated or chopped

200ml double cream

5 or 6 Cadbury Creme Eggs

few squares of milk chocolate, to finish

6. For the ganache, place the chocolate in a heatproof bowl. Heat the double cream to boiling point, then pour the cream over the chocolate. Leave to infuse for a few moments, then very carefully start to stir the mixture to combine the two until a ganache has formed. If you find there are still a few lumps of undissolved chocolate, you could use the heat from a hair dryer to complete the process. Try to avoid placing the ganache over direct heat or you will burn the chocolate.

7. Pour some of the ganache down the centre hole of the Bundt to create the floor of the nest. Leave this to set (it will take 3–4 hours), then transfer the remaining ganache to a piping bag fitted with a rosette piping nozzle. Pipe the ganache along the top of the cake, allowing some of it to run down the sides. Please note that some of the ganache will set inside the nozzle but this adds to the twiggy nest effect as it tries to squeeze out of the sides. Remove the foil from the Creme Eggs and carefully place them into the nest. Grate chocolate shavings over the whole cake. This cake will keep for up to 3 days if kept in an airtight tin; but my guess is that it won't last that long.

Catholics who have abstained from meat and eggs during Lent often find themselves with an abundance on Easter Day (the hens don't stop laying!). Happily, baking a cake is the perfect way to use them up. In Catalonia, a 'mona' cake is traditional. The origins of its name are not entirely clear but it's thought that 'mona' comes from the Moroccan word meaning 'gift'. It was the cake that godparents offered their godchildren on Easter Monday. Mona cakes were originally made with marzipan and hard-boiled eggs, with the number of eggs corresponding to the godchild's age (though no fewer than two and no more than twelve). This cake uses them in a light buttery sponge, and a rich eggy custard.

Lynn Hill
Founder of
Clandestine Cake Club

MONA CAKE

SERVES 8–10

4 large eggs

125g caster sugar

1 tsp vanilla paste

100g self-raising flour, sifted

50g unsalted butter, melted and cooled

2 heaped tbsp apricot preserve

50g flaked almonds, to decorate

CRÈME PATISSIÈRE

200ml double cream or whole milk, plus an extra 100ml double cream

1 vanilla pod, seeds scraped

60g caster sugar

2 large egg yolks

30g plain flour or cornflour

60g unsalted butter

1. Preheat the oven to 200°C/fan 180°C/gas 6. Grease the sides and base of two 18cm sandwich tins and line the bases with baking parchment.

2. Start by making the crème patissière. Pour the 200ml of cream or milk into a pan and add the vanilla pod and seeds. Over a low heat, bring the cream to just below boiling point to 'scald' it, then remove from the heat.

3. In a large bowl, whisk together the sugar, egg yolks and flour until well combined. Pour the vanilla-infused cream mixture through a sieve over the sugar mixture. Rinse out the pan, then pour the mixture back into it and cook gently over a low heat, whisking constantly to prevent any lumps forming. Once thickened, add the butter and stir until it has melted. Pour the crème patissière into a medium bowl, then cover the surface with cling film to prevent a skin forming. Chill immediately until needed.

4. Whisk the eggs, sugar and vanilla paste in a large heatproof bowl until well combined. Place the bowl over a pan of simmering water and whisk until pale in colour and thick enough to leave a trail when you lift the whisk. Remove the bowl from the pan and continue to whisk until thick and cool.

5. Gradually fold in half the flour using a large metal spoon or thin spatula. Pour the cooled melted butter around the edge of the bowl and fold in, very lightly cutting through the mixture, until it is well incorporated. Very carefully fold in the remaining flour. Pour the mixture into the prepared tins and bake for 20–25 minutes or until a skewer inserted in the centre of the cakes comes out clean. Leave to cool in the tins for a few minutes before gently turning out on to a wire rack to cool completely.

6. Once cool, sandwich the two layers together with the apricot preserve. You will need to loosen the crème patissière to be able to spread it so push the mixture through a sieve then stir to bring it together. Whip the extra 100ml of double cream until it just starts to thicken and hold its shape, then stir it into the crème patissière. Coat the whole cake with the crème patissière then cover with the almonds.

Lynn Hill
Founder of
Clandestine Cake Club

In April 2014, at a clandestine location in Leeds, a very special CCC event took place. I and several other bakers welcomed guest of honour Nigel Slater, who'd come with a film crew to take part in a Cake Club gathering for a documentary called *The Icing on the Cake*. This magnificent cake, topped and filled with caramel sauce and crowned with caramel buttercream, was the one that I chose to bake for the occasion. Clearly it hit the spot for Nigel and his crew – by the end of the event, not even a crumb remained! So it seems the perfect tribute with which to toast national treasure Nigel on his birthday.

SEA SALTED CARAMEL CAKE

SERVES 8–10

250g unsalted butter, softened

250g soft light muscovado sugar

60g salted caramel sauce (see recipe below, or use ready-made)

4 large eggs, beaten

250g self-raising flour

SALTED CARAMEL SAUCE

200g unsalted butter

200g dark muscovado sugar

1 level tsp sea salt, plus a little extra to finish

200ml double cream

20g dark chocolate (70 per cent cocoa solids), broken into pieces

> *Ingredients and recipe continue overleaf*

1. Start by making the salted caramel sauce. Melt the butter, sugar and salt over a low heat. Bring to a gentle simmer and leave for 5 minutes, stirring occasionally. Take off the heat and add the chocolate and then the cream. Mix until well combined, then set aside to thicken and cool.

2. Preheat the oven to 200°C/fan 180°C/gas 6. Grease and line two 20cm loose-bottomed cake tins.

3. Beat the butter and sugar using a wooden spoon or electric whisk, until light and fluffy. Measure out 60g of the cooled salted caramel sauce (or the ready-made version, if using). Mix until well combined.

4. Gradually add the beaten eggs with a little flour to help prevent curdling. Mix until well combined, then fold in the remaining flour.

5. Divide the batter between the cake tins and bake in the centre of the oven for 20–25 minutes or until a skewer inserted in the centre of the cakes comes out clean. Leave the cakes in the tins to cool for a few minutes before turning out on to a wire rack to cool completely. ❯

CARAMEL BUTTERCREAM

250g unsalted butter, softened

500g icing sugar, sifted

60g salted caramel sauce (see recipe on previous page) or use ready-made

2 tbsp double cream

6. Make the buttercream. Beat the butter and sugar until light and fluffy. Add the salted caramel sauce and cream then mix until well combined.

7. Sandwich the cakes together with a thin layer of the salted caramel sauce. Using a palette knife, cover the sides of the cakes with a very thin layer of the buttercream – a 'crumb coat'. The crumb coat gives you a good base on which to decorate your cake, catching any crumbs that may spoil the overall appearance of the cake. Leave in the fridge for 30 minutes to set.

8. Remove the cake from the fridge. Place the remaining buttercream in a piping bag fitted with a plain nozzle or star-shaped nozzle according to preference, then pipe swirls and whirls around the sides of the cake, finishing with two rings of swirls around the top of your cake.

9. Place the remaining salted caramel sauce into a disposable piping bag with the end snipped off to make a small hole. Pipe the caramel into the round in the centre of the top of the cake to create a pool and finish with a scattering of sea salt. Leave to set a little in the fridge before serving. This cake can be kept in the fridge up to 2 days.

Marked in over 100 countries, World Book Day is a wonderful celebration of books, authors and illustrators. In the UK its aim is to get children reading and to encourage excitement about books. At CCC we never pass up an excuse for cake, so Katherine has devised this beautiful book-shaped treat to mark the occasion. Gather your children, pop the kettle on and sit everyone down for story-time. Better still, theme the cake around a favourite book. Katherine's peach and caramel cake gives a nod to a famous fruit-filled classic by Roald Dahl, but go where your imagination takes you. There are so many wonderful cake decorating products available that you can really go to town in creating your edible book.

Katherine Bosiacki

PEACH AND CARAMEL BOOK CAKE

SERVES 20

280g unsalted butter, softened

280g caster sugar

6 medium eggs

300g self-raising flour (can be regular or gluten-free)

60ml semi-skimmed milk

¾ tsp vanilla extract

10 tsp peach melba instant tea powder (from Whittards of Chelsea) or any instant peach tea powder

FILLING AND ICING

200g Carnation ready-made caramel

600ml double cream

2–3 tbsp icing sugar, plus extra to dust

500g ready-to-roll white sugarpaste

writing gels, sprinkles, coloured sugarpaste, shimmer sprays etc., to decorate as you wish

1. Preheat the oven to 200°C/fan 180°C/gas 6. Grease and line two 32 x 23cm rectangular baking tins, leaving a 5cm overhang at end end.

2. Beat the butter and sugar using a wooden spoon or electric whisk until light and fluffy. Add the eggs one at a time, beating well after each addition, and adding a tablespoon of flour with the final egg to prevent curdling.

3. Mix together the milk, vanilla extract and tea powder, until the powder has dissolved. Pour into the creamed butter mixture and mix until combined. Fold in the remaining flour. Divide the mixture between the tins and level the surface. Bake in the oven for 15–20 minutes or until golden and a skewer inserted in the centre of the cakes comes out clean.

4. Remove from the oven and immediately use the paper to lift the cakes out of the tins on to wire racks.

5. Once cool, sandwich the cakes together with the caramel. Whip the double cream with the icing sugar (enough to suit your taste) to stiff peaks. Spread a very thin layer of the cream over the top of the sponge to create a 'crumb coat'. To mould some open pages in your book, turn the sponge so that the long sides are facing you. Spoon the cream into two mounds, one on each half of the book, running from the top of the sponge to the bottom.

6. Very lightly dust a work surface and rolling pin with icing sugar and roll out the sugarpaste until 4mm thick. Very gently lay the sugarpaste over the cream, then decorate the cake as you wish. You can write or draw text on the top using writing gels, make any other decorations using coloured sugarpaste to place as images on the book pages, or simply sprinkle or spray on sugar decorations or glitter. If you've chosen to use gluten-free flour, the cake is best eaten within 2 days.

Jessica Elmore

Her Majesty Queen Elizabeth II celebrates two birthdays each year: her actual birthday (21st April) and her official birthday, which is celebrated with public ceremonies in June. Rumours are rife as to the Queen's favourite cake: we know her 80th birthday was celebrated with a chocolate cake, but she is also thought to be partial to a honey and cream sponge. Jessica has taken matters into her own hands and designed a very special cake to celebrate the birthday of the longest lived monarch in British history in a colourful, beautifully British way.

CAKE FIT FOR A QUEEN

SERVES 10

120g salted butter, at room temperature

280g caster sugar

230g plain flour

2 tbsp cornflour

1 tbsp baking powder

3 large eggs

2 tsp vanilla extract

240ml full-fat milk

red gel food colouring

blue gel food colouring

CHEESECAKE LAYER

450g full-fat cream cheese

125g caster sugar

2 large eggs

150ml double cream

1½ tsp vanilla extract

1. Preheat the oven to 160ºC/fan 140ºC/gas 3. Grease and line a 23cm springform cake tin. Fill a roasting tin with water and place in the bottom of the oven – the moisture created by the heat in the oven will help stop the cheesecake layer cracking.

2. Start with the cheesecake layer. Beat the cream cheese till smooth, then beat in the sugar. Beat in the eggs, then mix in the cream and vanilla. Pour the mixture into the lined tin and bake for 40 minutes or until the cheesecake is set with a slight wobble in the middle. Allow to cool to room temperature in the tin, then place in the freezer for 5 hours or overnight.

3. Remove the tin of water from the oven and adjust the temperature to 180ºC/fan 160ºC/gas 4. Grease and line two 23cm loose-bottomed cake tins.

4. Beat the butter and sugar using a wooden spoon or electric whisk until light and fluffy.

5. Place the dry ingredients in a bowl and whisk together. In a separate bowl, do the same with the wet ingredients (not the colourings). Using an electric hand whisk or stand mixer, beat a third of the dry ingredients into the creamed butter and sugar on a low speed, then beat in half the wet ingredients, scraping the bowl as you go. Repeat these additions and finish by beating in the final third of dry ingredients. Spoon half of the mixture into another bowl and mix in a few drops of red colouring, adding enough to get a nice vivid colour. Repeat with the blue in the other bowl.

FROSTING AND DECORATION

250g salted butter, at room temperature

250g full-fat cream cheese

450g icing sugar

2 tsp vanilla extract

red, white and blue sprinkles, to decorate

6. Pour each batch of mixture into a prepared tin and bake for 30 minutes or until a skewer inserted in the centre of the cakes comes out clean. Remove from the oven and leave to cool in the tins for 5 minutes, then turn out on to a wire rack to cool completely.

7. For the frosting, beat the butter until creamy. Beat in the cream cheese but do not overbeat. Sift the icing sugar over the top in two batches, mixing well. Stir in the vanilla and beat until smooth and creamy.

8. To assemble, decide whether you want to start with red or blue, and place that cake layer on to a serving plate. Top with a little of the frosting and spread out with a palette knife. Take the cheesecake out of the freezer and remove the tin and lining, then position it on top of the first cake layer. Spread some frosting on the top and finally add the remaining cake layer. Use the rest of the frosting to cover the top and sides of the cake, smoothing it with the palette knife. Decorate with sprinkles.

Earth Day began in 1970 in the United States after a senator witnessed the widespread devastation left by a Californian oil spill. Inspired by the student anti-war movement he wanted to infuse the public with the same degree of energy about the need to protect our planet. He announced a day of mobilisation at which 20 million Americans stood up to demonstrate in favour of environmental awareness. Earth Day is now observed around the world by over a billion people and is a wonderful opportunity to support a cause that is so important for the future of our children. Baking this cake, which uses some of nature's most delicate and health-giving ingredients, is just one of the ways you can remind yourself of the value of our planet. In spring, the hedgerows are filled with climbing roses, which later produce their vibrant Vitamin C-rich rose hip fruits. Colourful crocus flowers yield one of the world's most expensive and delicate spices: saffron. And there is nothing more earthy than a ginger root, which we dig from the ground to add warmth and spiciness to our baking. (Pictured overleaf.)

Lynn Hill
Founder of
Clandestine Cake Club

SAFFRON, ROSE HIP AND GINGER CAKE

SERVES 10–12

50ml buttermilk

¼–½ tsp saffron threads

200g unsalted butter, softened

225g caster sugar

4 medium eggs, lightly beaten

225g self-raising flour, sifted

2 tbsp rose hip syrup

2 tbsp hot boiled water

1. Preheat the oven to 200°C/fan 180°C/gas 6. Grease and line two 20cm loose-bottomed sandwich tins.

2. Gently heat the buttermilk in a small pan with the saffron for just a couple of minutes, to help bring out some of the yellow colour. Do not allow to boil. Take off the heat and leave to cool completely, allowing the colour and flavour to infuse.

3. Beat the butter and sugar using a wooden spoon or electric whisk until light and fluffy. Slowly add the beaten eggs, beating well after each addition, and adding a tablespoon of flour to prevent curdling. Fold in the remaining flour followed by the infused buttermilk and mix until well combined.

4. Divide the mixture between the tins and bake for 20–25 minutes or until a skewer inserted in the centre of the cakes comes out clean. Leave in the tins to cool for 5–10 minutes before turning out upside down on to a sheet of greaseproof paper. Remove the lining from the bottom of the cakes.

5. Mix the rose hip syrup and hot water, then brush the mixture over the bottom of the cakes while they are still warm, then leave to cool completely.

FROSTING

350g full-fat cream cheese

¼ tsp saffron threads

350ml double cream

1 tbsp rose hip syrup

1 tbsp icing sugar, sifted (optional)

200g ready-made ginger preserve

pinch of saffron threads, to decorate

6. Make the frosting. Lightly beat the cream cheese to loosen it a little, then add the saffron and cream. Mix together until thick and creamy. Add the syrup, and icing sugar if you like a sweeter frosting, and mix until well combined. Set aside for a few minutes to allow the saffron to release its yellow colour a little.

7. Mix the frosting again to incorporate any leeched colour from the saffron. Place one cake layer on your favourite plate, syrup-side up (level any doming with a serrated knife if you need a straighter bottom for it to sit flat), then cover with a thin layer of frosting. Spread about 120g of the ginger preserve on top of the frosting, then top with the second cake layer.

8. Using a spatula or palette knife, cover the whole cake with a very thin layer of frosting – a 'crumb coat' – then place in the fridge for about 20 minutes to firm up a little.

9. Cover the cake with a full layer of frosting, then transfer the remainder to a piping bag fitted with your favourite rosette nozzle. Pipe two rings of stars around the edges of the top of the cake, leaving enough room in the centre on which to spread the remaining preserve. Decorate by placing a pinch of saffron threads in the middle.

Arguably the greatest writer in the English language, William Shakespeare's legacy includes 38 plays, 154 sonnets and various verses, which offer a fascinating glimpse into our history. Many of his symbols and metaphors are as meaningful today as they were then. One of these is the rose, which features especially in his sonnets. Now a symbol of romance, it was probably Shakespeare who first gave it this association, just as he is responsible for coining many words in the English language and some of our best-known quotes and phrases. The Rose was also the name of Shakespeare's first London playhouse, so this flower is a fitting flavour for a cake baked in his honour. Made by one of our youngest members, Myfanwy, her recipe combines rose with strawberries, another Shakespearian motif, notably in *Othello* and *Richard III*. It's a sweet tribute to a much-loved Briton.

Myfanwy Hywel

STRAWBERRY ROSE CAKE

SERVES 10–12

225g butter, softened and cubed

225g caster sugar

4 medium eggs

225g self-raising flour

1 tsp baking powder

RED CAKE LAYER

115g butter, softened and cubed

115g caster sugar

2 medium eggs

115g self-raising flour

1 tsp baking powder

red gel food colouring

1. Preheat the oven to 180°C/fan 160°C/gas 4. Grease and line two 20cm cake tins.

2. Beat the butter and sugar using a wooden spoon or electric whisk, until light and fluffy. Add the eggs one at a time, beating well after each addition, and adding a tablespoon of flour with the final egg to prevent curdling. Sift together the remaining flour and baking powder and gently fold in. Divide the mixture between the tins and level the surface. Bake for 20–25 minutes or until a skewer inserted in the centre of the cakes comes out clean. Leave the cakes in their tins for a few minutes then turn out on to a wire rack to cool completely.

3. For the red cake layer, grease and line a 20cm cake tin. Beat the butter and sugar using a wooden spoon or electric whisk until light, and fluffy. Add the eggs one at a time, beating well after each addition and adding a tablespoon of flour with the second egg to prevent curdling. Sift together the remaining flour and baking powder and gently fold in, then stir through enough red colouring until you have a bright red. Pour the mixture into the tin. Bake in the oven for 20–25 minutes or until a skewer inserted in the centre of the cake comes out clean. Leave in the tin for a few minutes then turn out on to a wire rack to cool completely. When cool, slice off a very thin layer around the outer edge of the cake. Crumble these pieces to make crumbs and set aside.

STRAWBERRY CREAM FILLING

800g strawberries, hulled, half
sliced and half left whole; keep a
whole one for decoration

450ml double cream

75g icing sugar, sifted

ROSE CREAM COVERING

450ml double cream

75g icing sugar, sifted

rose water, to taste

4. For the strawberry cream, whizz the unsliced strawberries in a blender. Pass the purée through a sieve to get rid of the seeds. Whip the double cream until it holds its shape. Using a metal spoon, fold the puréed strawberries into the cream, then fold in the icing sugar.

5. For the rose cream, whip the cream until it holds its shape. Carefully fold in the icing sugar with a metal spoon. Fold in a couple of drops of rose water and taste before deciding on whether to add another drop or two more (before re-tasting, take a sip of water to clear your taste buds).

6. To assemble, place one of the cooled plain cakes on a plate and spread half of the strawberry cream over it, then cover with half the sliced strawberries. Cover the underside of the second cake with a very thin layer of strawberry cream (this will help the cake to stick), then place on top and repeat the strawberry cream and sliced strawberry layer. Finally, cover the underside of the red cake layer with a very thin layer of strawberry cream, then place it on the top.

7. Using a palette knife, cover the sides and top of the cake with the rose cream, smoothing it down. Sprinkle the red cake crumbs around the top outer edge of the cake. Pop the whole strawberry on the top to decorate. This cake should be kept in the fridge and will last for up to 5 days.

MAY

1st May
MAY DAY
SPRING CITRUS CAKE

4th May
JAPANESE GREENERY DAY
MATCHA CHIFFON CAKE

5th May
CINCO DE MAYO
TEQUILA AND LIME CAKE

13th May
WORLD COCKTAIL DAY
COCONUT AND MOJITO
'TRES LECHES' CAKE

19th May
DAME NELLIE MELBA'S
BIRTHDAY (1861)
AMARETTINI
AND PEACH MELBA CAKE

23rd May
EUROVISION
SONG CONTEST
SMARTIE PANTS CAKE

24th May
QUEEN VICTORIA'S
BIRTHDAY (1819)
PLUM, LEMON
AND VANILLA CAKE

25th May
AFRICAN
LIBERATION DAY
MOCHA-CHOCA-RULA CAKE

27th May
JAMIE OLIVER'S
BIRTHDAY (1975)
GLUTEN-FREE
COURGETTE CAKE

Late May
CHELSEA FLOWER SHOW
CHELSEA FLOWER SHOW
CAKE

Spring Bank Holiday
COOPER'S HILL CHEESE
ROLLING
ORANGE CURD
CHEESECAKE

Lynn Hill
Founder of
Clandestine Cake Club

The 1st May, or May Day, harbours more reasons for a holiday than possibly any other date in the year. In many cultures it is Labour Day, a tradition that began in nineteenth-century USA when unions went on strike on this date, demanding that the working day be shortened. In Britain, however, it is a joyful celebration that marks the return of spring. Historically, festivities included gathering wild flowers, weaving garlands, crowning a May king and queen and plenty of dancing around a maypole. Such exertions definitely require sustenance and this citrus-flavoured cake, zingy with merriment, is just the ticket. Decorate it with a colourful maypole and ribbons made out of citrus peel; it is sure to be one of the 'darling buds of May'.

SPRING CITRUS CAKE

SERVES 10–12

220g self-raising flour

pinch of salt

4 medium eggs

280g caster sugar

80g unsalted butter, melted and cooled

120ml double cream

grated zest of 1 lime and 1 lemon

1½ tbsp mixture of lemon and lime juice

SYRUP

150ml water

75g caster sugar

pared zest of 1 lime and 1 lemon, cut into very fine matchsticks

50ml lemon juice

50ml lime juice

ICING (OPTIONAL)

50g icing sugar

juice of ½ lemon

1. Preheat the oven to 190°C/fan 170°C/gas 5. Grease and line a 20cm cake tin with a cake liner (especially if using a loose-bottomed tin).

2. Sift the flour and salt into a bowl and leave to one side. Beat the eggs and sugar for about 5 minutes, until pale and fluffy.

3. Gradually add the cooled melted butter, cream, citrus zest and juice and mix together until well combined. Fold in the flour and give it a good mix so that there are no lumps in the batter. Pour into the cake tin and bake for 40–45 minutes or until a skewer inserted in the centre of the cake comes out clean. Leave in the tin to cool.

4. Make the syrup. Place the water, sugar and citrus strips into a pan and simmer over a low heat until all the sugar has melted. Add the lemon and lime juice, turn up the heat a little and continue to simmer until the syrup has reduced by half. Take off the heat and leave to cool a little.

5. Make small holes in the cake with a skewer and pour the syrup with the lime and lemon strips over the top, arranging the strips attractively.

6. If icing the cake, place the icing sugar in a small mixing bowl and gradually add the lemon juice until a thick, slightly runny consistency is achieved. Pour the icing into a small piping bag and pipe it over the cake in a spiral petal-like pattern, or any way you wish.

Nancy Nim

Greenery Day, or Midori no hi, is a Japanese holiday dedicated to the environment and to thanking nature for its bounty. Tree plantings are held around the country, as are many events that bring people closer to nature, with parades, paper lanterns and fireworks adding energy to the festivities. Nancy's light-textured, matcha-flavoured cake is a fitting contribution to the green celebrations. The addition of this distinctive tea powder not only provides colour, it gives the sponge a unique bittersweet note that is characteristic of the Japanese tea. You can buy matcha in Asian supermarkets and online.

MATCHA CHIFFON CAKE

SERVES 10–12

150g plain flour

2 tbsp matcha powder

1 tbsp baking powder

9 medium eggs, at room temperature, separated

100g caster sugar

100ml vegetable or sunflower oil

200ml milk

1 tsp vanilla extract

½ tsp cream of tartar

ready-made white or green sugarpaste leaves, to decorate

WHITE CHOCOLATE GANACHE

200g white chocolate, broken into pieces

250ml double cream

1. Start by making the ganache. Put the white chocolate and 100ml of the double cream into a heatproof bowl. Place the bowl over a pan of simmering water, ensuring that the water doesn't touch the bowl. Stir until the chocolate has completely melted. Leave to cool at room temperature, then stir in the remaining cream. Chill for 1–2 hours or until it thickens.

2. Preheat the oven to 160°C/fan 140°C/gas 3. Have ready a 25cm non-stick angel food cake tin (do not grease it).

3. Sift together the flour, matcha powder and baking powder. Repeat.

4. In a bowl, whisk together the egg yolks and sugar until fluffy and well combined. Then whisk in the oil, milk and vanilla extract. Add the flour mixture to the egg yolk mixture and mix until well combined.

5. In a separate bowl, whisk the egg whites with the cream of tartar until stiff peaks form. Carefully fold a third of the egg white into the yolk mixture with a large metal spoon. Repeat, folding in a third of the egg white at a time.

6. Carefully pour the cake mixture into the cake tin and gently tap the bottom twice to remove any large air bubbles. Bake for 45–50 minutes or until a skewer inserted in the cake comes out clean. After the first 40 minutes of baking (don't open the oven any sooner), check the top of the cake to see if it's getting too brown or cracked too much. If this is the case, cover the top of the tin with foil and carry on baking.

7. Remove the cake from the oven, immediately turn it upside down and place on a wire rack. The cake needs to be completely cool before you remove it from the tin. Leave to cool for at least 1 hour.

8. To remove, run a palette knife around the outer and inner edges of the ring and gently push the cake out of the tin. You may need to even the base to get it to sit straight.

9. Once the ganache is ready, generously spread it on top of the cake, letting it run down the sides. Decorate with the sugarpaste leaves or make your own using ready-to-roll sugarpaste.

For Mexicans, the 'cinco de mayo' (5th May) commemorates their militia's victory over the French army at the Battle of Puebla in 1862. Having gained independence from the USA in 1821, it marked an important triumph during a period of troubled history and is still seen as cause for a party. The day is primarily a regional holiday, celebrated most prominently in the state of Puebla, but the festivities have spread along the US–Mexican border and in fact are now more popular north of the border where the day has become a celebration of Mexican music, food and drink. Serving a cake laced with a shot of the nation's famous alcoholic export is the perfect way to kick off a Mexican fiesta in honour of the occasion. Have your limes at the ready and – for an authentic touch – don't forget to rim your Margarita glasses with salt or sugar.

Joanne Hodgson

TEQUILA AND LIME CAKE

SERVES 10

200g unsalted butter, softened

200g caster sugar

3 large eggs

200g self-raising flour

50ml milk

2 tbsp tequila

2 tbsp lime juice

GLAZE

100g icing sugar

2 tsp lime juice

2 tsp tequila

1–2 tsp vanilla extract (optional)

grated lime zest or multi-coloured sprinkles to decorate

1. Preheat the oven to 160°C/fan 140°C/gas 3. Grease and line a 20cm deep-sided cake tin.

2. Beat the butter and sugar using an electric whisk, until light and fluffy. Add the eggs one at a time, beating well after each addition, and adding a tablespoon of flour with each egg to help prevent curdling. Stir the milk, tequila and lime juice into the mixture. Very gently fold in the remaining flour – this mixture really wants to curdle!

3. Pour the mixture into your prepared cake tin and bake in the centre of the oven for 45 minutes or until a skewer inserted in the centre of the cake comes out clean. Leave to cool in the tin for a few minutes, then turn out on to a wire rack to cool completely.

4. To make the tequila and lime glaze, sift the icing sugar into a bowl. Stir in the lime juice and tequila. The glaze will have quite a kick to it but if it is too sharp for your liking, then add the vanilla extract to take away the sharpness.

5. Pour the glaze over the cake and spread to ensure it covers the top. Decorate with some grated lime zest or multi-coloured sprinkles – whichever you prefer.

Sam Smith

Cocktail and mocktail themed events are very popular with Cake Club members who shake and stir all manner of ingredients to turn their favourite tipple into a cake. Sam has created a South American-inspired 'tres leches' cake – sponge soaked in three milks: condensed milk, evaporated milk and double cream – which is infused with the punchy flavours of the traditional Cuban rum cocktail, the mojito. It's perfect for sharing on World Cocktail Day, which celebrates the day in 1806 when the word 'cocktail' was first put into print, thereby officially recognising the alchemy of mixing spirits.

COCONUT AND MOJITO 'TRES LECHES' CAKE

SERVES 10–12

250g plain flour

1½ tsp baking powder

½ tsp salt

150g unsalted butter, softened

250g caster sugar

6 large eggs

natural coconut flavouring

grated zest of 1 lime

TRES LECHES GLAZE

200g evaporated milk

200g condensed milk

75ml double cream

100ml ready-made mojito cocktail mix

TOPPING

600ml double cream

75g icing sugar, sifted

75g desiccated coconut

1. This cake is best made and soaked the night before you need it so it gives time for the flavours to develop and to let the liquid soak into the cake. Preheat your oven to 180°C/fan 160°C/gas 4. Grease and line two 20cm loose-bottomed cake tins.

2. In a bowl, sift the flour, baking powder and salt together. In another bowl, beat the butter and sugar using a wooden spoon or electric whisk, until light and fluffy. Add the eggs one at a time, beating well after each addition, and adding a tablespoon of the flour mixture with each egg to help prevent curdling. Add the remaining flour then add a few drops of coconut flavouring and fold in the lime zest.

3. Divide the mixture equally between the tins and bake in the oven for 20–25 minutes, until a skewer inserted in the centre of the cakes comes out clean. Leave to cool in the tins for 30 minutes (they should still be slightly warm at this stage).

4. To make the tres leches glaze, mix the evaporated milk, condensed milk, double cream and mojito mixture in a large jug. Prick the top of the cakes all over with a skewer but leave them inside the tins. Pour the glaze in equal measures carefully over the two cakes. Put them in the fridge overnight (still in the tins) so that the liquid will soak in.

5. The next day, make the topping. Whip the double cream with the icing sugar. Put one of the cake layers carefully on a plate, then cover it thickly with some of the cream. Top this with the second layer then spread the remaining cream on top of the cake. Sprinkle with the desiccated coconut.

Dame Nellie Melba, born Helen Porter Mitchell, rose from a provincial childhood in Australia to become one of the most famous opera singers of her day. Known for being rather a diva but with a commanding stage presence and a beautiful voice, Melba was one of the biggest celebrities of the early twentieth century, loved by fans around the world. So adored was she that the famous French chef Auguste Escoffier created a dessert in her honour, called after the stage name she'd adopted (Melba being short for her home town of Melbourne). Traditional peach Melba is simply fresh peaches served with raspberry purée and vanilla ice cream, but a birthday cake for a dame requires a touch more glamour so this recipe takes its cue from the famous dessert and adds a note of sophistication, with almond sponge, white chocolate buttercream, peach slices and freeze-dried raspberries.

Lynn Hill
Founder of
Clandestine Cake Club

AMARETTINI AND PEACH MELBA CAKE

SERVES 8

115g unsalted butter, softened

115g caster sugar

2 large eggs

115g self-raising flour

few drops of almond extract

20g amarettini biscuits, crushed

BUTTERCREAM TOPPING

150g white chocolate, grated or chopped

1 x 400g can peaches in natural juice, drained but reserve 4 tbsp of juice

200g unsalted butter, softened

75g icing sugar, sifted

1 tbsp freeze-dried raspberries

1. Preheat the oven to 200°C/fan 180°C/gas 6. Grease the sides and line the base of a 20cm loose-bottomed sandwich tin.

2. In a large bowl, beat the butter and sugar using a wooden spoon or electric whisk, until light and fluffy. Lightly beat the eggs and add them a little at a time, with a little flour, to the buttery mixture. Mix until well combined, then fold in the remaining flour. Add the almond extract and crushed amarettini and mix until well combined.

3. Pour the batter into the tin and bake on the middle shelf of the oven for 25 minutes or until a skewer inserted in the centre of the cake comes out clean. Leave in the tin to cool for 20 minutes before turning out on to a wire rack to cool completely.

4. While the cake is cooling, make the white chocolate buttercream. Place the white chocolate in a heatproof bowl. Heat the peach juice in a pan and when hot pour this over the chocolate. Do not stir at this point, but leave to infuse and allow the chocolate to melt for a few minutes.

5. Beat the butter and icing sugar together with an electric whisk, until light and creamy. Amalgamate the chocolate and peach juice together by gently stirring from the centre of the bowl with a spoon. With the mixer running, slowly pour the chocolate into the buttercream and beat until well combined. Pour into a piping bag fitted with a plain nozzle and leave in the fridge for around 15 minutes to firm up a little.

6. Now assemble the cake. If your sponge has a slight dome to it, turn it over so that you have an even, flat surface. Pipe the buttercream on top so that it resembles petals. Sprinkle the freeze-dried raspberries over the buttercream before topping with the peaches, arranging them in a circle and pointing them outwards in the same direction as the tips of the petals. This cake will only keep for 1–2 days in the fridge because of the fruit.

Ruth Tebbutt

The first Eurovision Song Contest was broadcast in May 1956 and it has since become one of the longest running TV shows in the world. Up to 43 countries participate, and the winning country qualifies as the host for the following year. Eurovision is a very popular theme for CCC events, with members often choosing to make a cake representing a participating nation. Rather than pick sides, Ruth has created a cake that reflects the colourful spirit of the event and the kaleidoscope of cultures, characters and costumes that viewers have come to expect. With such an entry, there's no fear of getting 'nul points'!

SMARTIE PANTS CAKE

SERVES 12–15

175g self-raising flour

1½ level tsp baking powder

2 tbsp good-quality cocoa powder

¼ tsp salt

75g caster sugar

75g soft dark brown sugar

150ml milk

150ml vegetable oil

2 large eggs

2 tbsp golden syrup

½ tsp vanilla paste or extract

10 x tubes Smarties

2 x packets milk chocolate fingers

CHOCOLATE FUDGE BUTTERCREAM

90g butter

60g cocoa powder

3 tbsp golden syrup

few drops of vanilla paste or extract

5 tbsp milk

375g icing sugar, sifted

1. Preheat the oven to 180°C/fan 160°C/gas 4. Grease and line two 20cm cake tins.

2. Sift all the dry ingredients into a large bowl and stir with a spoon. If the brown sugar will not sift, rub it through your fingers to make sure there are no lumps. Make a well in the centre.

3. Place all the wet ingredients (including the vanilla) in a measuring jug and mix briefly. Tip the wet ingredients into the well in the dry. Using an electric whisk or balloon whisk, beat all the ingredients together until combined, but don't overbeat. Scrape the sides and bottom of the bowl and whisk again briefly.

4. Divide the mixture equally between the tins and bake for 25 minutes, or until the cakes spring back when pressed lightly in the middle. Don't open the oven door before 20 minutes is up. Leave in the tins to cool for 10 minutes, then run a knife round the edges and turn the cakes out on to a wire rack to cool completely.

5. Meanwhile, separate the Smarties by colour and set aside.

6. Place all the buttercream ingredients, except the milk and icing sugar, in a pan set over a very, very low heat. Stir until completely melted, then remove from the heat, add the milk and stir again. Sift in the icing sugar and beat with a fork until all lumps are gone. Put the buttercream aside for 15–20 minutes to set.

7. Sandwich the two cakes together with a third of the buttercream, then cover the top of the cake with a third and the sides of the cake with the remaining third. Arrange the chocolate fingers all around the cake as shown in the photograph. You need to do this while the buttercream is still a little soft. Stand the Smarties pointing upwards on the top of the cake, pressing them in gently. Start in the middle and work outwards in circles, using a different colour for each circle. You could tie a ribbon around the chocolate fingers for a nice finishing touch.

Charlotte Lightbody

The Victorians are well known for their love of all things sweet, so it follows that one of the most beloved and baked cakes in Britain should be named after the monarch who lends the era her name. You'll find a recipe for a classic Victoria sandwich on page 149, but to commemorate Queen Victoria's birthday, Charlotte has chosen to celebrate her other legacy to the food world's vernacular: the Victoria plum. The bright red fruit was discovered by a Sussex gardener the year the monarch was crowned and so he named it after her. Here, plums are the crowning glory in a sweet, light vanilla sponge cake – a fitting tribute to a cake-loving queen.

PLUM, LEMON AND VANILLA CAKE

SERVES 10–12

150g unsalted butter, softened

175g caster sugar

2 medium eggs

175g self-raising flour

grated zest of 1 lemon

1 tsp vanilla paste

125ml buttermilk or full-fat milk

1 x 570g can plums in syrup, drained

15–20g flaked almonds

1. Preheat the oven to 180°C/fan 160°C/gas 4. Grease a 20cm springform cake tin and line the base.

2. Beat the butter and sugar using a wooden spoon or electric whisk, until light and fluffy. Add the eggs one at a time, beating well after each addition, and adding a tablespoon of flour with the final egg to prevent curdling.

3. Mix in the lemon zest and vanilla, then gently stir in the buttermilk and the remaining flour until evenly combined. Do not overmix. Spoon the batter into the prepared tin and smooth the top.

4. Arrange the plums on top, cut-side up, then scatter over the flaked almonds. Bake for 50–60 minutes, until the cake is set and golden; the fruit will sink into the cake as it cooks.

5. Leave to cool in the tin for 20 minutes, then turn out on to a wire rack to cool completely.

In 1958, the leaders of eight African countries met at the first Conference of African Independent states to discuss collaboration in freeing Africa from foreign rule. The day continues to be marked every year and has become known as African Liberation Day. Lucianne's safari-themed cake was inspired by a visit to South Africa where she discovered the local mocha-choca-rula drink, a rich, creamy concoction of hot chocolate, coffee and Amarula liqueur. Amarula is made from the exotic marula fruit, a juicy yellow-skinned fruit that grows only on the sub-Saharan plains. The fruit is distilled until it becomes a spicy, vanilla-flavoured alcohol and is then mixed with cream to create the hugely popular liqueur (which is widely available in supermarkets in the UK). All the flavours and fragrance of that South African holiday are captured in this cake to commemorate this important day.

Lucianne Quinn

MOCHA-CHOCA-RULA CAKE

SERVES 10–12

150g unsalted butter, softened

275g golden caster sugar

2 tbsp coffee essence (or dissolve 3 tbsp good-quality instant coffee granules in 1 tbsp of boiled water and leave to cool)

2 tbsp white wine vinegar

200ml milk

60g self-raising flour

185g plain flour

1 tsp bicarbonate of soda

60g cocoa powder

3 large eggs

1. Preheat the oven to 180°C/fan 160°C/gas 4. Grease and line two 23cm sandwich tins.

2. Beat the butter and sugar using a wooden spoon or electric whisk, until light and fluffy. Mix in the coffee essence. In a separate jug, briefly stir the vinegar and milk. Finally, in a separate bowl, sift together the flours, bicarbonate of soda and cocoa powder.

3. Add the eggs to the creamed butter and sugar, one at a time, beating well after each addition, and adding a tablespoon of the flour mixture with the final egg to help prevent curdling. Beat in the remaining flour until just incorporated before adding the milk and vinegar mix. Again beat until just combined before dividing the mixture between the tins.

4. Bake for 20–30 minutes on the lower shelf of the oven, until a skewer inserted into the centre of the cake comes out clean and the sponge is starting to pull away from the sides of the tin. Leave to cool in the tins for 25 minutes before transferring to a wire rack to cool completely.

5. Make the frosting. Beat the butter until light and fluffy before adding a third of the icing sugar. Beat until incorporated and then add the remaining icing sugar in two more batches, beating well between each. Finally, add the Amarula and coffee essence and beat for 5 minutes, until smooth, fluffy and light. Adjust the amounts of coffee and Amarula to suit your taste if you prefer one flavour stronger than the other.

FROSTING

250g unsalted butter, softened

500g icing sugar, sifted

3 tbsp Amarula cream liqueur,
or to taste

2½ tbsp coffee essence
(see opposite for alternative),
or to taste

brown gel food colouring
(optional)

black gel food colouring
(optional)

6. Once the sponges are completely cool, use a palette knife to sandwich the cakes with some of the frosting, then cover the whole cake with a very thin layer of frosting – a 'crumb coat'. Set aside for 20–30 minutes, then cover with a full layer of frosting (you should have frosting left over for decorating).

7. After smoothing off the frosting and leaving it to set a little, take the end of a piping nozzle or something similar with a hole in and press it over the whole cake to give a dappled effect.

8. Colour a third of the remaining buttercream with a few drops of black gel food colouring and the remainder with brown. Fit a piping bag with a thin round nozzle, fill with the black buttercream and start to pipe random misshapen kidney and oblong shapes of various sizes – just the outlines – over the cake (like a leopard or cheetah print). Wash the nozzle.

9. Transfer the brown buttercream to a piping bag fitted with the clean nozzle, and once the black outlines have started to set, pipe the brown buttercream into each one to fill the shapes. Once the shapes have started to set, rough them up a little with the end of the nozzle or a toothpick to give a lined/furry effect.

Gemma Johnson

Not only a hugely successful chef and cookery book writer, Jamie Oliver is famous for his pioneering work in educating children about where their food comes from, how to grow and cook it and above all inspiring them to eat healthily. So, in honour of Jamie's birthday, Gemma has created a 'healthy twist' on a cake, which she thinks even the campaigning chef would approve of. You will have no problems sneaking at least one of their five-a-day into your children's tummies with her deliciously moist, spiced courgette cake, packed with pukka green goodness.

GLUTEN-FREE COURGETTE CAKE

SERVES 12–14

200g soft light brown sugar

180ml vegetable oil

60g Greek yoghurt

3 large eggs, at room temperature

2 tsp vanilla extract

500g gluten-free plain flour

1 tsp bicarbonate of soda

2 tsp ground cinnamon

¼ tsp ground nutmeg

½ tsp ground mixed spice

½ tsp salt

260g courgettes, grated, plus 20g extra to decorate

100g mixed raisins

CREAM CHEESE FROSTING

115g unsalted butter, at room temperature

225g cream cheese, at room temperature

300g icing sugar, sifted

2 tbsp double cream

2 tsp vanilla extract

pinch of salt

1. Preheat the oven to 190°C/fan 170°C/gas 5. Grease and line the base of a 23cm cake tin.

2. Using an electric whisk, mix the brown sugar and oil in a bowl on a medium speed until well combined. Add the yoghurt and mix for a further minute until the ingredients come together. Add the eggs one at a time, beating well after each addition. Just before adding the last egg, mix in the vanilla extract. Set this bowl aside.

3. Sift the flour, bicarbonate of soda, cinnamon, nutmeg, mixed spice and salt into another large bowl and stir to combine. Fold the grated courgette into the wet ingredients, then add the dry ingredients to the bowl and mix in using a low speed on the electric whisk. Lastly fold in the dried raisins.

4. Pour the batter into the cake tin and bake for 40–50 minutes on the middle oven shelf, until a skewer inserted in the centre of the cake comes out clean. Leave in the tin for 10 minutes, then turn out on to a wire rack to cool completely.

5. To make the frosting, use an electric whisk to beat the butter on a slow speed until creamy. Add the cream cheese and continue to beat on a medium speed for 2–3 minutes until creamy, fluffy and combined. Add the icing sugar and beat until the mixture is thick. Add the double cream, vanilla extract and salt and beat on a medium speed for 2 minutes. Once the cake is cool, spread the cream cheese frosting thickly over the top. Decorate with a scattering of grated courgette.

Towards the end of May gardening enthusiasts and flower fanatics flock to south-west London to attend the Royal Horticultural Society's world-famous Chelsea Flower Show. Over 500 exhibitors compete to win one of the prestigious medals, treating visitors to a magnificent array of floral and outdoor garden displays. In honour of the burgeoning blooms, here is a real petal of a celebration cake: a three-layered tier of delicate floral-flavoured sponges, covered with buttercreams to match, and topped off with pretty sugarpaste flowers. You could even paint a sugarpaste disc with edible gold lustre to award your cake a medal of its own!

Karen Waller

CHELSEA FLOWER SHOW CAKE

SERVES 20

350g unsalted butter, softened

350g caster sugar

6 large eggs, beaten

350g self-raising flour

1 tsp baking powder

½ tsp vanilla extract

½ tsp violet flavouring

½ tsp rose water

ready-made sugarpaste flowers, to decorate

VANILLA BUTTERCREAM

100g unsalted butter, softened

200g icing sugar, sifted

1 tsp milk

½ tsp vanilla extract

1. Preheat the oven to 180°C/fan 160°C/gas 4. Grease and line three 20cm sandwich tins.

2. Beat the butter using an electric whisk. Gradually add the caster sugar to the butter and mix until light and fluffy. Add the eggs one at a time, beating well after each addition, and adding a tablespoon of the flour mixture with the final egg to help prevent curdling. Sift the remaining flour and baking powder together and add to the mixture, beating until combined.

3. Divide the sponge mix into three and put each third into a separate bowl. Mix the vanilla into one bowl, the violet into another and the rose water into the third. Be careful with the violet and rose and add them slowly, checking the flavour as you go, as different brands vary in strength. Mix well.

4. Pour into the tins and bake in the oven for 20–25 minutes, until the sponges are golden in colour and a skewer inserted in the centre of each cake comes out clean. Leave in the tins for a few minutes to cool then turn out on to wire racks to cool completely.

VIOLET BUTTERCREAM

100g unsalted butter, softened

200g icing sugar, sifted

1 tsp milk

violet flavouring, to taste

few drops of violet gel food colouring

few Parma Violets sweets, crushed to a fine powder (optional, but use these if you want a stronger violet flavour)

ROSE BUTTERCREAM

200g unsalted butter, softened

400g icing sugar, sifted

1 tbsp milk

rose water, to taste

few drops of pink gel food colouring

5. While the cakes are cooling, you can make the buttercreams. The method for each buttercream is the same: beat the butter until creamy. Gradually mix in the sifted icing sugar. When thoroughly combined, add the milk, then the flavouring (add the violet flavouring and rose water very slowly, tasting as you go) and finally the colouring (again, in drops until your desired colour is achieved). Beat well until mixed.

6. The cake can then be assembled. Place the violet-flavoured sponge on a plate or cake stand. Using a palette knife, cover the top and sides of the sponge with the violet buttercream. Carefully put the vanilla sponge on top. If necessary, trim off any excess sponge on the cakes so that they are straight when stacked. Cover the top and sides of the vanilla sponge with the vanilla buttercream. Then place the rose water sponge on top. Cover the sides and top with the rose buttercream. To get a more even finish, try placing the frosted cake in the fridge for an hour or two and then spread a second layer of each buttercream on the cake. Decorate with the sugarpaste flowers.

Note

To create a gold medal as an additional decoration, roll a ball of ready-to-roll white sugarpaste and flatten it to form the shape of a medal. Mix a few drops of an alcohol-based flavouring with gold edible lustre and paint on to the sugarpaste using a pastry brush until it is evenly coloured gold. Leave to dry and harden for a day.

Named after the hill on which it takes place, Gloucestershire's annual cheese rolling festival finds hundreds of competitors gathering at the top of the steep slope before hurtling down it in pursuit of a hefty Double Gloucester cheese. Happily, there is nothing heavy or hazardous about Charlotte's creamy orange cheesecake, which she created in honour of the festival, nor is there any need to roll down a hill to enjoy it. With its zingy orange curd topping, you can savour your cheese in a far more sedate fashion. Be sure to allow plenty of time for the cheesecake to chill fully or it will be too soft.

Charlotte Pike

ORANGE CURD CHEESECAKE

SERVES 8–10

350g full-fat cream cheese

100g caster sugar

450g double cream

grated zest of 1 navel orange, to decorate

ORANGE CURD

grated zest and juice of 2 navel oranges

grated zest and juice of 1 lemon

200g caster sugar

100g unsalted butter

3 eggs

BISCUIT BASE

12 digestive biscuits

80g unsalted butter, melted

1. Lightly grease and line a 20cm springform cake tin and set aside.

2. Start by making the curd. Place all the ingredients apart from the eggs in a heatproof bowl set over a pan of simmering water. Ensure the bottom of the bowl does not touch the water. Whisk the mixture well to combine, then add the eggs. Continue to stir as the curd gradually thickens; it will take 20–30 minutes. When the curd is thick enough to coat the back of a spoon, it's ready (it will continue to thicken as it cools). Allow to cool completely before making the cheesecake.

3. Next, make the base. Place the biscuits in a plastic food bag and bash using a rolling pin until the biscuits resemble fine sand. Place in a mixing bowl and stir in the melted butter. Tip this mixture into the prepared tin and flatten it down evenly to cover the base. Set aside.

4. Make the cheesecake mixture by beating together the cream cheese and sugar. Add the cream and beat until thick, then gently fold in half the curd.

5. Spoon the cheesecake mixture over the biscuit base and level out. Cover with cling film and refrigerate overnight.

6. The next day, slowly pour the remaining curd over the cheesecake. Gently spread it over the cake, then cover and refrigerate again for at least 4 hours . When you're ready to serve, release the cake by running a knife around the edge of the tin, scatter over the orange zest and serve immediately.

JUNE

June
RASPBERRY SEASON

RASPBERRY
CAPPUCCINO CAKE

6th June
NATIONAL DAY
OF SWEDEN

SWEDISH
SANDWICH CAKE

Mid June
ETON AND HARROW
CRICKET MATCH

ETON MESS CAKE

24th June
MIDSUMMER'S DAY

SUMMERY LEMON
AND MINT CAKE

Late June
FATHER'S DAY

GINGER AND STOUT CAKE

Late June
GLASTONBURY FESTIVAL

GLUTEN-FREE BUCKWHEAT,
CARROT AND SULTANA CAKE

Late June
BAKEWELL CARNIVAL

CHERRY BAKEWELL CAKE

Late June
WIMBLEDON TENNIS
FORTNIGHT

STRAWBERRY PIMM'S CAKE

Katherine Howe

Bursting with vital vitamins and natural sweetness, British raspberries are one of the highlights of the summer season. They are a popular ingredient with CCC bakers and often take the starring role in a wide variety of cakes. Tired of the usual raspberry partnerships, such as with white chocolate, mixed berries or cream, Katherine wanted to try something a little different with these beloved fruits. She created the perfect pick-me-up by whipping her berries into a coffee-flavoured sponge. The fruity notes in the roasted coffee complement the ripe berries beautifully.

RASPBERRY CAPPUCCINO CAKE

SERVES 10–12

4 tbsp double cream

2 tbsp instant coffee granules

225g unsalted butter, softened

110g golden caster sugar

110g white caster sugar

4 medium eggs

150g raspberries

225g self-raising flour

1 tsp baking powder

RASPBERRY BUTTERCREAM

75g unsalted butter, softened

300g icing sugar

50g raspberries, plus a few whole, to decorate

1. Preheat the oven to 190°C/fan 170°C/gas 5. Grease and line two 20cm sandwich tins.

2. Warm the cream in a small pan. Once at boiling point, remove from the heat, add the coffee and stir until dissolved. Set aside to cool.

3. Beat the butter and sugars using a wooden spoon or electric whisk, until light and fluffy. Add the eggs one at a time, beating well after each addition. Add the cool coffee cream and mix well.

4. Place the raspberries in another bowl with the flour and baking powder. Tip this mixture into a sieve and sift over the beaten batter; this helps dredge the raspberries in flour without using any extra. Beat in the flour until well mixed, then tip in the raspberries; don't overmix or you will squash them.

5. Divide the mixture between the tins and bake for 20–25 minutes or until a skewer inserted in the centre of the cakes comes out clean. Leave in the tins for 5–10 minutes before turning out on to wire racks to cool completely.

6. To make the buttercream, use an electric hand whisk to mix the butter and icing sugar together. When it has the consistency of soft sand, add half the raspberries. Mix again and it will quickly come together. Add the remaining raspberries and lightly mix so you get some large bits of fruit in the buttercream. Depending on how juicy your raspberries are, you may need to add a few drops of water.

7. Once the cakes are cool, spread half the buttercream over the bottom layer of cake, cover with the second sponge and spread the remaining buttercream over the top. Decorate with whole raspberries.

It is a little surprising that such an upstanding establishment could have wanted to serve an untidy dessert, but Eton mess, the muddle of crushed meringue, strawberries and cream, was invented by the prestigious Eton College and is the dessert traditionally served to players and spectators at their annual cricket match against the pupils of Harrow School. You will definitely bowl everyone over with this tribute to the quintessential English pud: a light sponge, striking meringue crown, crushed strawberry cream and white chocolate chunks make it the perfect celebratory finish to a picnic on the lawn.

Clare Conlon

ETON MESS CAKE

SERVES 10–12

225g margarine

225g golden caster sugar

4 medium eggs

225g self-raising flour

1½ tsp baking powder

MERINGUE

2 medium egg whites

120g caster sugar

1 tsp cornflour

1 tsp white wine vinegar

BUTTERCREAM

160g unsalted butter, softened

500g icing sugar

4–6 tbsp milk

> *Ingredients and recipe continue overleaf*

1. Preheat the oven to 180°C/fan 160°C/gas 4. Grease and line two 20cm sandwich tins.

2. Beat the margarine and sugar using an electric whisk until light and fluffy. Crack the eggs into a jug and give them a quick beat with a fork.

3. Sift the flour and baking powder into a bowl and stir together, then add about half to the margarine and sugar mixture. Mix on a slow speed then slowly add the egg mixture. Beat in the remaining flour mixture; making sure you scrape the bottom and sides of the bowl so it is all combined.

4. Divide the mixture between the tins and place in the oven for 25 minutes or until a skewer inserted in the centre of the cakes comes out clean. Once the cakes are out of the oven, decrease the setting to 160°C/fan 140°C/gas 3.

5. Leave the cakes in their tins for 10–15 minutes, then turn out on to a wire rack to cool completely. Lay a sheet of baking parchment on a tray and draw round the shape of your 20cm cake tin.

6. Make the meringue by whisking the egg whites in a bowl until stiff. Add the sugar a teaspoon at a time while continuing to whisk. In a separate small dish, stir together the cornflour and vinegar, then whisk into the meringue mixture.

7. Fill a disposable piping bag with the meringue mixture and snip off the end. Pipe a series of connected blobs within the circle shape you have drawn but give the ring on the outer edge a little more height (pipe it as if you were making the meringue nest for a pavlova). Pipe any leftover meringue in random blobs around the free part of the baking parchment (these can be any shape or size as they will be broken into pieces later). >

DECORATION

2–3 tbsp raspberry jam

50g white chocolate chunks

100g strawberries, roughly chopped, plus a few left whole

50g raspberries, roughly chopped, plus a few left whole

8. Place the meringue in the oven and immediately turn it down to 150°C/fan 130°C/gas 2 and bake for 40–45 minutes. Once cooked the meringue should be a creamy, very light brown colour and the shell will be firm to the touch. Leave to cool in the oven with the door closed for an hour or two for a chewier meringue.

9. To prepare the buttercream, place the butter, icing sugar and 4 tablespoons of the milk in a mixing bowl or the bowl of a stand mixer. Cover with a tea towel to avoid an icing sugar cloud and beat until smooth and mousse-like; this usually takes a good 5 minutes. Add more milk, a little at a time, if required.

10. To assemble the cake, spread a layer of buttercream over the bottom sponge, followed by a generous helping of jam.

11. Pop the odd bits of meringue in a sandwich bag and give them a light bash with a rolling pin – not too much as you do want some chunks. Sprinkle a thin layer of meringue pieces over the jam and then scatter over some of the white chocolate chunks.

12. Place the second layer of sponge on top and spread it with a very thin layer of buttercream. Gently take the large meringue and stick it on top.

13. Stir the strawberries, raspberries and leftover meringue pieces into the remaining buttercream – the amount is entirely up to you depending on your preference. Stir the fruit in very gently as you don't want the raspberries to turn to a pulp. Spoon this mixture on to the top of the meringue in the centre and add some whole berries and the remaining white chocolate chunks.

Swedes are not generally known for their displays of national pride but every year on the 6th June they take to the streets and wave their flags in celebration of the date they achieved independence and founded their kingdom. Smörgåstårta (sandwich cake) is a popular (savoury!) Swedish staple commonly served at parties, brunches and afternoon teas. The filling varies but usually involves some kind of smoked fish, cucumber and dill, all sandwiched together with a creamy filling between layers of bread. Vivienne made her smörgåstårta for a picnic-themed event at her Cake Club event in Voorschoten. Once you've got your head around the idea of biting into a savoury cake, you can sit back and enjoy the light, fresh ingredients of her delicious no-bake recipe. It's the perfect antidote to the sugar rush that so often accompanies an afternoon tea, or most CCC events!

Vivienne Brodrick

SWEDISH SANDWICH CAKE

SERVES 10–12

1–2 loaves of coarse-textured bread, depending on size

1 tbsp butter, softened

100g smoked salmon slices

5 tsp mild mustard

5 tsp sunflower oil

handful of shredded lettuce

2 large eggs, hard-boiled and cooled

3 tbsp mayonnaise

salt and freshly ground pepper

TOPPING

300g cream cheese

1–2 tbsp plain yoghurt

1 tbsp lemon juice

thinly sliced cucumber, to decorate

dill fronds, to decorate

small cooked prawns, to decorate

1. Cut the bread into three circles, each about 18cm in diameter and 2–3cm thick. Use a bread knife and a side plate or the insert from a springform baking tin as a guide.

2. Butter the bottom layer, then lay the smoked salmon on top. Mix the mustard with the sunflower oil and spread on top of the salmon. Then sprinkle on the shredded lettuce. Cover with the second layer of bread.

3. Mash the hard-boiled eggs with the mayonnaise and some salt and pepper, to taste. Spread this egg mixture on the second layer of bread. Place a third layer of bread on top.

4. Mix the cream cheese with a bit of the yoghurt and some of the lemon juice to give a firm spreading consistency; exact quantities will depend on how firm the cheese is.

5. Do a final trim of the cake if necessary to make the top and sides as smooth as possible. Spread the topping over the top and sides, as if spreading icing. Decorate the top with thinly sliced cucumber, dill and prawns, if wished. Chill until needed. The cake will keep in the fridge for 1–2 days.

Lindsey Barrow

About 1,500 people paid £1 to watch Marc Bolan headline the first 'Pilton Pop Festival' in 1970; spectators were handed free milk from the local farm and a cultural legend was born. The Glastonbury festival (as it was later renamed) has exploded to become one of the biggest festivals in the world, welcoming around 200,000 visitors each year, for five days of music, dance, art, theatre, poetry and everything in between. It is a mainstay of the British summer calendar and tickets sell out within hours. If you're not lucky enough to get your hands on a pass, why not stage your own festival, complete with this wholesome carrot cake inspired by the event's earthy, outdoor beginnings.

GLUTEN-FREE BUCKWHEAT, CARROT AND SULTANA CAKE

SERVES 8–10

100g sultanas

3–4 tbsp orange juice, with pulp and ideally freshly squeezed

175g buckwheat flour (check it's gluten-free; not all are)

2 tsp baking powder

1 tsp ground cinnamon

½ tsp ground cloves

½ tsp freshly grated nutmeg

3 medium eggs

150ml coconut oil, melted, or sunflower oil

200g soft light brown sugar

3 carrots, finely grated

carrot ribbobs, grated carrot or chopped nuts, to decorate (optional)

BUTTERCREAM

125g unsalted butter, softened

250g icing sugar, sifted

1. Preheat the oven to 180°C/fan 160°C/gas 4. Grease and line the base of two 22cm sandwich tins.

2. Put the sultanas and orange juice into a small pan, bring to a gentle simmer for 2–3 minutes, then remove from the heat and leave to cool. This will encourage the sultanas to soften and plump up. Drain once cool, reserving the orange juice for the buttercream.

3. Sift the flour, baking powder and ground spices into a mixing bowl.

4. In a separate bowl, whisk the eggs, oil and sugar until smooth and paler in colour. Add the carrot and drained sultanas, then quickly fold in the flour and spice mixture.

5. Pour into the prepared tins, dividing the mixture as equally as possible and smoothing the top. Bake in the oven for 25 minutes until a skewer inserted in the centre of the cakes comes out clean. Remove from the oven and leave to cool in the tins.

6. To make the buttercream, beat the butter, icing sugar and reserved orange juice together, ideally using a stand mixer, until you have a smooth, fluffy buttercream. Once it has come together beat for at least 6 minutes more so that the icing sugar has time to melt into the butter.

7. To ice and fill the cake, remove the cooled cakes from their tins. Smear a little of the buttercream on to your cake plate/stand and place the first layer of the cake on top. Now fill with half the buttercream mixture, using a palette knife to spread the buttercream to the edges. Top with the second cake, gently pressing the two layers together. Cover with the remaining buttercream. The cake can be decorated with nuts, carrot ribbons, grated carrot or served just as it is. If you need to transport the cake, first place it in the fridge to firm it up.

If you were to bottle the flavours of a British summer, you would most likely end up with a glass of Pimm's. The tawny-coloured gin-based spirit, mixed with water and served ice-cold with a garnish of citrus, cucumber, strawberries and mint, is the very embodiment of all things summery (if you need further confirmation turn to page 110 for the stats on just how much of it is consumed at Wimbledon each year). So, to celebrate Midsummer's Day, Jen has whisked the ingredients of the famous cocktail into this zingy lemon and mint cake, finished with a generous soaking of Pimm's syrup. Easily transportable, it's perfect for afternoon teas in the garden, picnics in the park or even a trip to Stonehenge to mark the solstice.

Jen Barber

SUMMERY LEMON AND MINT CAKE

SERVES 8–10

175g unsalted butter, softened

175g caster sugar

3 large eggs

200g self-raising flour, sifted

grated zest of 1 lemon and the juice of 2 lemons

generous handful of chopped mint

PIMM'S DRIZZLE

3 tbsp Pimm's

2 tbsp lemon juice

2 tbsp Demerara or granulated sugar

1. Preheat the oven to 180°C/fan 160°C/gas 4. Grease and line a 900g loaf tin.

2. Beat the butter and sugar with an electric hand whisk, until light and fluffy. Add the eggs one at a time, beating well after each addition, and adding a tablespoon of the flour mixture with the final egg to help prevent curdling. Add the lemon zest and fold in the remaining flour using a metal spoon, followed by the lemon juice and mint. Transfer the mixture to the tin and bake for 40–50 minutes, until golden.

3. While the cake is baking, make your drizzle by mixing the Pimm's, lemon juice and sugar.

4. When the cake comes out of the oven, make holes all over the top with a cocktail stick or skewer and pour over the drizzle. Leave to cool in the tin, so the drizzle can sink into the cake. Once cool, turn out on to a cake plate to serve.

Bethan Carter

Having celebrated motherhood in March; in June it's our fathers' turn to put their feet up and be spoiled for a day. Even if your dad isn't typically a stout drinker, he is sure to love the gentle malty hops flavour and sweet, rich dark molasses in this cake. And with its simple buttercream filling and fine dusting of icing sugar, it's light and modest enough for Dad to kick back a little bit longer and enjoy a second slice.

GINGER AND STOUT CAKE

SERVES 8–10

250ml stout

350g molasses

2 tsp baking power

2 medium eggs

230g dark muscovado sugar

110g margarine

250g self-raising flour

1 tbsp ground ginger

2 tsp ground cinnamon

BUTTERCREAM

140g unsalted butter, softened

250g icing sugar, sifted,
plus extra for dusting

1–2 tsp milk

2–3 tbsp shredless marmalade

1. Preheat the oven to 200°C/fan 180°C/gas 6. Grease and line two 20cm round tins.

2. Combine the stout and molasses in a pan and bring to the boil. Remove from the heat, add the baking powder and allow to foam and then settle.

3. Whisk the eggs and sugar until thick and pale. Add the margarine, flour and spices and whisk again to combine. Finally stir in the stout mixture, then divide the batter evenly between the tins.

4. Give each tin a few stirs with a fork then bake for 30–35 minutes, until firm and a skewer inserted in the centre of the cakes comes out clean. Leave to cool in the tins for 10–15 minutes, then turn out on to a wire rack to cool completely.

5. For the buttercream, beat the butter, and gradually add the icing sugar and milk until thick and well combined. Add a little more icing sugar if needed.

6. To assemble, spread the marmalade over one cake layer, then cover it with the buttercream and then the second cake. Dust the top of the cake with icing sugar.

Bakewell in Derbyshire is best known for its eponymous (and slightly controversial) dessert, but once a year thousands descend on the market town to enjoy a week of events leading up to its carnival day. The carnival queen is crowned and a colourful procession of floats parades through Bakewell's streets. In the dessert, a simple almond filling sits on a layer of jam. The controversy is in the name. Traditionalists will tell you that it was originally called a 'pudding' and made with a flaky pastry base; these days it is more commonly made with a shortcrust bottom and called a tart. Celebrate carnival day but avoid the debate with this Bakewell-inspired cake instead, a fragrant almond sponge sandwiched with cream and cherry jam.

Julie O'Brien

CHERRY BAKEWELL CAKE

SERVES 8–10

200g unsalted butter, softened

200g caster sugar

4 large eggs

100g self-raising flour

100g ground almonds

1 tsp baking powder

½ tsp almond extract

pinch of salt

FILLING AND TOPPING

450ml double cream

175g icing sugar, plus 4 tbsp

150g morello cherry conserve

100g flaked almonds, toasted

60g dark chocolate (70 per cent cocoa solids), melted

100g glacé cherries

1. Preheat the oven to 180°C/fan 160°C/gas 4. Grease and line the base of two 20cm sandwich tins.

2. In a large bowl, beat the butter and sugar using a wooden spoon or electric whisk, until light and fluffy. Add the eggs one at a time, beating well after each addition, and adding a tablespoon of flour with the final egg to help prevent curdling. Add the remaining flour, then the rest of the ingredients and beat until smooth.

3. Spoon into the tins and level the tops. Bake for 30 minutes or until golden and springy. Take care not to open the oven door before 25 minutes has passed. Allow to cool in the tins for 5–10 minutes, then turn out, peel off the baking parchment and leave to cool completely on a wire rack.

4. In a clean bowl, whip the double cream with the 4 tablespoons of icing sugar until stiff.

5. Place one sponge on a serving plate and spread with the conserve. Spread the other sponge half with a quarter of the whipped cream before sandwiching the two together. Using a spatula or palette knife, gently spread the remaining cream around the sides of the cake, filling any ridges or uneven surfaces as you go. Cover the sides of the cake with the flaked almonds.

6. Sift the 175g of icing sugar into a clean bowl, then gradually add water until you have a thick, smooth icing. Pour the mixture on to the top of the cake, covering all of the naked sponge. Pour the melted chocolate into a piping bag fitted with your smallest round nozzle (or snip a tiny hole off the end of a disposable piping bag). Working fairly quickly, pipe thin lines of chocolate across the cake, around 2cm apart. Run a toothpick across the lines at 2cm intervals, alternating the direction each time to create the trademark feathered effect.

7. Decorate with the glacé cherries. Due to the fresh cream this cake is best eaten on the day it's made, though it can be kept in the fridge for up to 2 days.

The annual Wimbledon Championships are the oldest tennis tournament in the world and the only one still to be played on a lawn, the game's original surface. Wimbledon fortnight is steeped in tradition, from the strict dress code for the players to the attendance of the royal family and the all-important menu. Estimates suggest that 28,000 kilograms of English strawberries and 7,000 litres of cream are consumed by spectators over the two weeks, washed down with 230,000 glasses of Pimm's! This cake is the perfect 'grand slam' to see you through the nail-biting action: two Pimm's-soaked sponges, filled and topped with ripe, juicy strawberries mixed with lashings of double cream; truly British summer at its best. All that remains is to keep your fingers crossed there's no rain to hold up play…

Lynn Hill
Founder of
Clandestine Cake Club

STRAWBERRY PIMM'S CAKE

SERVES 10–12

25g plain flour

55g cornflour

½ tsp baking powder

260g ground almonds

180g caster sugar

5 medium eggs

180g unsalted butter, melted and cooled

1½ tbsp Pimm's

PIMM'S SYRUP

90g caster sugar

1 pared strip of lemon zest (use a potato peeler)

½ vanilla pod, split in half lengthways

80ml Pimm's

1. Start by making the syrup. Put the sugar and lemon zest in a saucepan with 110ml of water. Add the vanilla seeds and empty pod and boil for 3 minutes. Take off the heat and add the Pimm's, then leave to cool.

2. For the chocolate-covered strawberries, place the chocolate in a heatproof bowl set over a pan of simmering water until the chocolate has melted. Take off the heat and leave to cool a little.

3. Dip each strawberry into the chocolate then place on a sheet of greaseproof paper to set while you make your cake.

4. Preheat the oven to 190°C/fan 170°C/gas 5. Grease and line the base and sides of a 20cm springform cake tin.

5. Sift together the flour, cornflour and baking powder several times until well combined.

6. Beat the ground almonds, sugar and eggs for 5 minutes. Gradually fold in the dry ingredients until thoroughly combined, then slowly add the cooled butter and the Pimm's and mix until well combined. Pour the mixture into the cake tin and bake for 45–55 minutes or until a skewer inserted in the centre of the cake comes out clean. Remove from the oven and leave to cool in the tin for a few minutes before turning out on to a wire rack to cool completely.

MASCARPONE FILLING

250g mascarpone

2 tbsp icing sugar, sifted

100ml double cream

2 tbsp Pimm's

200g strawberries, cleaned, hulled and halved

CHOCOLATE-COVERED STRAWBERRIES

100g dark chocolate (minimum 60 per cent cocoa solids), broken into pieces

12 strawberries, cleaned and hulled

7. Once cool, slice the cake in half horizontally and brush the Pimm's syrup over the cut side of each layer.

8. Make the filling. Beat the mascarpone and icing sugar. Add the double cream and 1 tablespoon of the Pimm's and beat until well combined. Add the remaining tablespoon of Pimm's to the strawberries and toss until coated.

9. Spread a third of the mascarpone mixture over the bottom layer of sponge, then top with all the Pimm's-soaked strawberries before adding the top sponge layer. Spread a very thin layer of mascarpone mixture on to the top, transfer the remainder to a piping bag fitted with a rosette nozzle (size 2D) and pipe large swirls around the outer top edge of the cake, filling the centre with smaller swirls. Arrange the chocolate strawberries on top, not forgetting to add one in the centre. This cake can be kept for up to 2 days in the fridge.

JULY

1st July
CANADA DAY

BACON AND
MAPLE SYRUP CAKE

4th July
INDEPENDENCE DAY

INDEPENDENCE DAY
CAKE

6th July
INTERNATIONAL
KISSING DAY

PINK BUBBLES AND
ROSE BUNDT CAKE

Early July
HENLEY ROYAL REGATTA

STRAWBERRIES AND CREAM
CHEESECAKE

Early July
INTERNATIONAL
MANGO FESTIVAL

MANGO AND
WHITE CHOCOLATE CAKE

17th July
OPENING OF FIRST
BETTYS TEAROOM (1919)

CARAMEL PECAN BRITTLE
SWISS ROLL

18th July
NELSON MANDELA'S
BIRTHDAY (1918)

CAPE BRANDY CAKE

Late July
SUMMER HOLIDAYS

GLUTEN-FREE ORANGE
SUNSHINE CAKE

Canada's national day commemorates the anniversary of when two British North American colonies were joined with the province of Canada to become a single independent country. It is a public holiday and Canadians celebrate it in as many different ways as they can, with barbecues, parades, fireworks and free street concerts. As the producer of more than 71 per cent of the world's maple syrup, this natural sweetener is an important export for the nation. For bakers, it's a wonderful ingredient, with a rich treacle-like flavour that gives cakes richness and depth without being overly sweet. The partnership of maple syrup and bacon is better known as a pancake topping but – unusual as it may sound – it also works brilliantly in a cake. Like peanut butter and jelly, or cheese and fruit, the classic combination of sweet and salty is timeless because it so deliciously moreish. Fire up your grill and get your bacon crispy, ready to celebrate Canada's national day.

Michelle Titmus

BACON AND MAPLE SYRUP CAKE

SERVES 8–12

about 18 slices of smoked streaky bacon (preferably dry-cured)

300g unsalted butter, softened

300g golden caster sugar

5 medium eggs

300g self-raising flour

1 tbsp milk (preferably full fat, but semi-skimmed is fine)

3 tbsp pure maple syrup (avoid any with carob syrup which dilutes the flavour)

FILLING AND TOPPING

250g unsalted butter, softened

500g icing sugar

3 tbsp maple syrup, plus extra for drizzling

1. Under a very hot grill, cook the bacon until crispy. Cook it directly on the grate so the fat drains easily – this helps the crisping process. Once cooked leave to cool on kitchen paper to drain off any excess fat.

2. Preheat the oven to 190°C/fan 170°C/gas 5. Grease and line the base of three 20cm sandwich tins.

3. Beat the butter and sugar using a wooden spoon or electric whisk, until light and fluffy. Add the eggs one at a time, beating well after each addition, and adding a tablespoon of the flour with the final egg to help prevent curdling. Add the milk and maple syrup and finally fold in the remaining flour a little at a time making sure it's well combined.

4. Take 10 slices of the cooled bacon and chop/rip/crumble them into smallish pieces and stir into the cake batter. At the same time you can chop/rip/crumble the remaining 8 slices and leave to one side ready for decoration.

5. Divide the cake mixture evenly between the three tins and bake in the oven for 20–25 minutes, until a skewer inserted in the centre of the cakes comes out clean. Leave to cool for about 10 minutes in the tins before turning out on to wire racks to cool completely.

6. To make the buttercream, mix the butter, icing sugar and maple syrup together until smooth and creamy, adding a spoon of slightly cooled boiling water if it is too thick or needs help to become smooth.

7. To assemble, level off any domed cakes so they stack evenly. Toss the bacon pieces in a drizzle of maple syrup to make them glossy. Spread some of the buttercream on top of the bottom cake then scatter on some of the drizzled bacon before placing the next cake on top. Repeat again on the next cake and again with the top cake, finishing with a drizzle of maple syrup on top of the scattered bacon, if you wish.

Breanna Sampson

The Fourth of July, as it is widely known, commemorates when the United States declarared independence from Great Britain and is one of America's biggest national holidays, with supersized celebrations to match. Decorating everything in red, white and blue is a common theme and this includes food, particularly desserts. This celebratory cake embraces the idea without resorting to artificial gels and dyes. Instead the colours come from fresh summer berries, using their natural colour as purées to tint and flavour the sponges and buttercreams. It's a colourful, multi-layered and patriotic tribute to the festivities.

INDEPENDENCE DAY CAKE

SERVES 12

3½ large egg whites, at room temperature

1 tbsp pure vanilla extract

½ tsp almond extract

250ml milk, at room temperature

400g cake or plain flour, sifted

300g caster sugar

20g baking powder

pinch of salt

170g unsalted butter, at room temperature

fresh strawberries and blueberries, to decorate

FRUIT PURÉES

340g strawberries, sliced (use frozen sliced strawberries if fresh are unavailable)

340g blueberries (use frozen if fresh are unavailable)

1. Start by making the fruit purées. Place a small saucepan over a medium heat and add the strawberries. Cook for 5 minutes, stirring occasionally. Pour the strawberries into a blender and mix until they become a completely smooth liquid with no lumps. Pour the purée through a sieve back into the pan. Continue to cook over a medium heat until the purée begins to simmer. Reduce the heat to medium–low and cook for 25 minutes, stirring frequently. When ready, it should be reduced by half and thickened. Repeat the same process with the blueberries. Let your finished purées cool to room temperature before you begin preparing the cake batter.

2. Preheat the oven to 175°C/fan 155°C/gas 4. Grease and flour two 20cm sandwich tins.

3. With a fork, stir together the egg whites, both extracts and 60ml of the milk in a small bowl. Set aside.

4. Mix the flour, sugar, baking powder and salt together in the bowl of a stand mixer. Keeping the mixer on a low speed, add the butter and drizzle in the rest of the milk. Beat for 10 seconds, then increase the speed to medium for 30 seconds. Stop and scrape down the sides of the bowl and beater with a rubber spatula. Add half the egg white mixture and continue to mix on a medium speed for 30 seconds. Stop and thoroughly scrape the bowl. Pour in the remaining egg white mixture, and again mix for 30 seconds on a medium speed.

5. Remove half the finished batter and place in a bowl. Gently fold half the strawberry purée into the bowl of batter and mix thoroughly. Do not overmix – you are aiming for a marbled batter, not a homogenous one. Scrape this batter into one of the prepared tins.

6. Fold half the blueberry purée into the remaining batter and pour this into the second tin.

FROSTING

350ml double cream, at room temperature

230g cream cheese, at room temperature

120g icing sugar, sifted

1 tsp pure vanilla extract

7. Bake for 35–40 minutes or until a skewer inserted in the centre of the cake comes out clean. Allow to cool in the tins for 10 minutes before turning out on to wire racks. When the cakes are completely cool, level the tops and cut each cake into two layers.

8. For the frosting, place the stand mixer bowl and beater attachment into the refrigerator for 20 minutes. Pour the double cream into the chilled bowl and beat on a high speed until it forms stiff peaks. Scrape the cream into another bowl and set aside.

9. Next, put the cream cheese into the empty mixer bowl. Whisk on a medium speed until there are no lumps and it is completely smooth. Scrape down the sides and add the icing sugar and vanilla. Mix until fully incorporated. Fold in the whipped cream until thoroughly combined.

10. Remove 100g of frosting and place in a small bowl. Add the reserved strawberry purée and fold in gently until combined. Repeat the process separately with another 100g of frosting and the reserved blueberry purée.

11. To assemble, place a layer of the blueberry cake on to a serving platter. Evenly spread the blueberry frosting on top of this layer. Top with the other blueberry half. Spread a layer of the remaining plain frosting on top, then cover with a layer of the strawberry cake. Spread the strawberry frosting on this layer. Place the final strawberry cake on top. Use the remaining plain frosting to cover the top and sides of cake. Decorate with strawberries and blueberries and serve immediately, or keep refrigerated until ready to serve.

Rachel McGrath

Believe it or not, International Kissing Day is an annual event that appreciates the humble kiss. The record for the longest kiss was set in 2005 in the UK at 31 hours and 30 minutes. It has since been broken several times and it now stands at 58 hours, 35 minutes and 58 seconds, which was achieved in 2013. After such an achievement, champagne and cake are most definitely called for. The bubbles in this sponge give it a wonderful sugary crust and perhaps the best thing about it is that you won't need the whole bottle to make the cake, so you'll have a few glasses of fizz to sip alongside your slice.

PINK BUBBLES AND ROSE BUNDT CAKE

SERVES 12–16

cake release spray, for the tin

225g unsalted butter, at room temperature

100g solid vegetable fat (such as Trex), at room temperature

650g golden caster sugar

5 large eggs, beaten

460g plain flour

¼ tsp salt

250ml good-quality pink champagne, cava or prosecco, plus a few tbsp for the icing

¼ tsp rose extract

pink gel food colouring

500g icing sugar

1. Preheat the oven to 180°C/fan 160°C/gas 4. Spray a 25 x 7cm Bundt tin with cake spray and dust with flour.

2. Beat the butter and vegetable fat with an electric whisk until creamy. Add the sugar and beat on a medium speed for about 5 minutes. Add the eggs one at a time, beating well on a slow speed after each addition.

3. Sift the flour and salt into a bowl. Mix the champagne and the rose extract in another.

4. Fold a third of the flour mixture into the creamed butter, then add half the rose-flavoured bubbles. Continue folding in the two mixtures alternately until they are all incorporated, then add a little pink food gel. Beat the mixture for about 10 seconds on a medium speed, then pour into the prepared tin.

5. Bake in the oven for 1½ hours. If it's not shrinking away from the sides of the tin at this point, leave it in for another 10–15 minutes; this is a big cake so it needs to be cooked for a long time on a low heat. Don't worry if the crust is brown; it should be – that's the caramelised sugar and tastes fantastic. Leave the cake to cool in the tin for 10 minutes before turning out on to a wire rack.

6. Once cool, add enough champagne to your icing sugar to make a runny icing, then pour it generously over the cake.

Henley Royal Regatta is a hugely popular sporting and social event dating back to 1839. It has enjoyed royal patronage since 1851, and is still frequented by the royal family. Over five nail-biting days, competitors from around the world row their boats down the Thames to try and win one of the 20 coveted trophies. While you can't take your own picnic into the Regatta enclosure, there's usually plenty of food on offer, with no shortage of strawberries and cream! For those without a ticket, here's a strawberries-and-cream cheesecake to recreate that racing spirit. Rest assured there won't be any sinking of boats after a slice of something so deliciously light.

Charlotte Pike

STRAWBERRIES AND CREAM CHEESECAKE

SERVES 8–10

350g full-fat cream cheese

100g caster sugar

1 tsp vanilla extract

450g double cream

BISCUIT BASE

12 digestive biscuits

80g butter, melted

TOPPING

300g strawberries, hulled and thinly sliced lengthways

icing sugar, to dust

1. Lightly grease and line a 20cm springform cake tin.

2. Start by making the base. Place the biscuits in a plastic food bag and bash using a rolling pin or similar implement until the biscuits resemble fine sand. Place the biscuit into a mixing bowl and stir in the melted butter. Tip this mixture into your prepared tin and flatten it down evenly to cover the base of the tin. Set aside.

3. Beat together the cream cheese, sugar and vanilla. Add the cream and beat until thick. Spoon the cheesecake mixture over the base and level out. Cover with cling film and refrigerate overnight.

4. Arrange the sliced strawberries over the cheesecake and dust with icing sugar. Serve immediately.

Lynn Hill
Founder of
Clandestine Cake Club

In many parts of the world, the start of the mango season signals the beginning of summer, and no more so than in India where a love of this tropical fruit borders on national obsession. There are thousands of varieties of Indian mango, and every year in Delhi, a two-day International Mango Festival celebrates and showcases the succulent sweet fruit, offering visitors the chance to savour different varieties. There are mango-eating competitions, mango carving sessions, children's shows and plenty of other entertainment. Why not contribute a British slant to the festivities by doing a spot of baking? Lightly toasted desiccated coconut and a white chocolate buttercream complement the fresh mango in this light and fruity summer cake.

MANGO AND WHITE CHOCOLATE CAKE

SERVES 8–10

225g unsalted butter, softened

225g caster sugar

1 tsp vanilla paste

4 medium eggs, lightly beaten

225g self-raising flour

2 tsp milk

FILLING AND FROSTING

250g white vanilla-flavoured chocolate

280g full-fat cream cheese

1 ripe mango, peeled and halved

1 tbsp desiccated coconut, lightly toasted

1. Preheat the oven to 180°C/fan 160°C/gas 4. Grease and line the base of two 20cm sandwich tins.

2. Beat the butter and sugar using a wooden spoon or electric whisk until light and fluffy. Add the eggs one at a time, beating well after each addition, and adding a tablespoon of flour with each egg to prevent curdling.

3. Beat in the vanilla paste and milk, then fold in the remaining flour and mix until well combined. Bake in the oven for 20–25 minutes or until a skewer inserted in the centre of the cake comes out clean. Leave in the tins for 5–10 minutes before turning out on to a wire rack to cool completely.

4. Melt the chocolate in a heatproof bowl over a pan of simmering water, without letting the bowl touch the water. Take off the heat and leave to cool.

5. With an electric whisk, lightly beat the cream cheese, then gradually add the cooled chocolate and keep mixing until well combined and smooth.

6. To assemble, spread a little of the frosting over one cake layer. Roughly chop one of the mango halves and arrange half on top of the frosting. Top with the second cake. Using a spatula or palette knife, cover the whole cake with a very thin layer of frosting – a 'crumb coat' – then place in the fridge for about 20 minutes to firm up a little. Cover the whole cake with the remaining frosting. Decorate the cake with the remaining mango half – chopped or sliced, then scatter the coconut over the mango. Because of the fresh fruit, this cake needs to be stored in the fridge and will keep for 1–2 days.

Lynn Hill
Founder of
Clandestine Cake Club

A Swiss baker named Frederick Belmont opened the first Bettys Tea Room in 1919, though the reason behind his chosen name remains a mystery. Today Bettys boasts six tea rooms around Yorkshire, serving exquisite cakes ranging from chocolate tortes and praline éclairs to Yorkshire tea loaves and their famous fat rascals. In honour of the opening of one of the finest tea rooms in England, here is an exquisite Swiss Roll honouring its founder's origins and artisan skills.

CARAMEL PECAN BRITTLE SWISS ROLL

SERVES 8

3 medium eggs, separated

140g soft light brown sugar

1 vanilla pod, seeds scraped

30g caster sugar

100g self-raising flour, sifted

CARAMEL PECAN BRITTLE

100g caster sugar

20g pecan nuts, roughly chopped

FILLING AND TOPPING

180g full-fat cream cheese

30g icing sugar, sifted

1 vanilla pod, seeds scraped

200ml double cream

20g pecan nuts, roughly chopped

12 pecan halves, to decorate

1. First, make the caramel pecan brittle. Line a baking sheet with baking parchment. Put the sugar and 35ml of water into a heavy-bottomed pan and gently heat until the sugar has dissolved. Bring the syrup to a boil until it begins to turn a golden caramel colour. Keep watching it. Remove from the heat and carefully add the chopped nuts. Give the pan a swirl – don't stir, making sure the nuts are coated in the caramel, then pour on to the baking parchment allowing it to find its own level. Leave to set and cool completely.

2. When cool, break the brittle into chunks before blitzing in a food processor until you have fine crumbs. Leave to one side until required.

3. Preheat the oven to 180°C/fan 160°C/gas 4. Grease and line a 32 x 23cm Swiss roll tin.

4. Beat the egg yolks, brown sugar and vanilla seeds using a wooden spoon or electric whisk, until thick and creamy and much lighter in colour.

5. In a clean bowl, whisk the egg whites until soft peaks form. Continue whisking as you slowly add the caster sugar until you have stiff peaks. Gently fold a little of the egg white into the yolk mixture to loosen it, then fold in two thirds of the egg white, then the flour and finally the remaining egg white.

6. Carefully pour the batter evenly into the tin and bake for 8–10 minutes or until a skewer inserted in the centre comes out clean. Leave in the tin to cool for a few minutes, then place a fresh sheet of baking parchment on top of the sponge and turn it out. Remove the old parchment. Beginning at the shorter end, roll up the sponge, including the paper. Leave rolled until it is cool.

7. Make the filling. Mix the cream cheese, icing sugar and vanilla seeds. In a separate bowl, whip the cream until soft peaks form. Gradually add this to the cream cheese mixture and mix until combined. Do not overmix.

8. Unroll the sponge, leaving it laid out on the baking parchment, then spread half the filling over it. Scatter over the chopped pecans, followed by a large handful of the crushed brittle. Starting with the shorter end, and with the aid of the baking parchment, start to roll the sponge around the filling. Place the remaining filling in a piping bag fitted with a rosette nozzle and pipe rosettes on top of the roll. Scatter more brittle over the whole cake and decorate with the pecan halves.

Duanne Hiscock

Nelson Mandela, often described as the 'Father of the Nation', is highly respected and honoured not only in South Africa but around the world. He gained international recognition for his activism and received more than 250 honours, including the Nobel Peace Prize. In 2009, his birthday was officially declared 'Mandela Day', a day to promote peace and to celebrate his legacy. As a fitting tribute to such a man, here's an adaptation of the Cape Brandy Tart, a favourite dessert in South Africa (the word 'tart' is misleading as it's a fruity date pudding, not dissimilar to Christmas pudding), reinvented as a rich cake topped with a brandy-flavoured mousse, which adds a different texture and lightens it.

CAPE BRANDY CAKE

SERVES 10–12

1 honeybush teabag

190ml boiling water

200g dates, chopped

1 tsp bicarbonate of soda

35g unsalted butter, softened

240g granulated sugar

1 large egg

245g plain flour

4 tsp baking powder

pinch of salt

30g pecan nuts, chopped

1. Preheat the oven to 180°C/fan 160°C/gas 4. Grease a deep-sided springform 23cm cake tin and line with foil.

2. Add the teabag to the boiling water and allow to steep for 2 minutes. Remove the bag and pour the hot tea over the dates and bicarbonate of soda. Allow to cool.

3. In a large bowl, beat the butter, sugar and egg using a wooden spoon or electric whisk, until light and creamy.

4. In a separate bowl, sift together the flour, baking powder and salt. Beat the dry ingredients into the creamed butter in thirds, alternating it with the date and tea mixture. Stir in the nuts.

5. Pour the mixture into the tin and bake for 45–55 minutes, until a skewer inserted in the centre of the cake comes out clean. Allow to cool in the tin. Once cool, remove from the tin and trim to achieve a nice flat top.

6. For the mousse, line a second 23cm springform cake tin with cling film.

7. In a saucepan over a medium heat, mix the sugars and 235ml of water, stirring to dissolve. Add the raisins, honey and molasses and bring to the boil. Boil for 5 minutes without stirring. Remove from the heat and add the brandy, butter and vanilla extract and stir to combine. Allow to steep for 20 minutes, then strain the liquid from the raisins, reserving both.

MOUSSE

70g granulated sugar

145g soft dark brown sugar

240g raisins

1 tbsp clear honey

1 tbsp molasses

125ml brandy

1 tbsp unsalted butter

1 tsp vanilla extract

5 gelatine leaves

500ml double cream

DECORATION

100ml double cream

8–12 glacé cherries

edible gold lustre (optional)

8. Place the gelatine in cool water and allow to soften for 5 minutes. Warm the reserved raisin liquid then remove the gelatine from the water and squeeze out the excess water. Stir the softened gelatine into the raisin liquid and stir until dissolved. Allow to cool again until thick, but not set.

9. Whisk the double cream until stiff peaks form. Add a third of the gelatine mixture to the cream and use a whisk to fold through. This will help to 'loosen' the cream. Add the remaining gelatine mixture to the whipped cream and fold through with the whisk so that no lumps of cream remain. Pour the mixture into the tin lined with cling film and place in the fridge to set for at least 6 hours but ideally overnight.

10. To assemble the cake, place the sponge on top of the mousse (still in its tin). Run a warm palette knife around the inside of the rim to help release the mouse and then invert the whole cake on to a cake plate. Release the mousse tin and carefully remove the cling film. If the appearance of the mousse seems irregular, heat a palette knife in hot water, wipe dry and run this around the mousse. This will help give you a smooth finish. Sprinkle the reserved raisins over the top of the mousse.

11. To decorate, whip the cream until it holds its shape. Either pipe or spoon rosettes or blobs of cream on to the cake and top each with a glacé cherry. For added glamour, sprinkle a little edible gold lustre over the top.

At last – the summer has arrived, school is out, and it's time for holidays, relaxing and getting together with family and friends. Summer baking calls for light afternoon treats to be enjoyed in the garden with refreshing accompaniments, and this delicate and versatile citrus cake is the perfect offering. Gill has chosen to use a gluten- and wheat-free flour but this can be substituted with plain flour if you're not baking for somebody with an intolerance. Ice-cold home-made lemonade would round off this summer celebration beautifully.

Gill Hepburn

GLUTEN-FREE ORANGE SUNSHINE CAKE

SERVES 10–12

170g unsalted butter, softened

170g caster sugar

3 medium eggs

170g gluten- and wheat-free flour, sifted (such as Doves)

grated zest of 2 oranges

2 tbsp milk

1 tsp gluten-free baking powder

½ tsp xantham gum

Jelly Tots, to decorate

ORANGE BUTTERCREAM

45g unsalted butter, softened

140g icing sugar

2–3 tbsp orange juice

1. Preheat the oven to 170°C/fan 150°C/gas 3. Grease and line two 18cm sandwich tins.

2. Beat the butter and sugar using a wooden spoon or electric whisk, until light and fluffy. Add the eggs one at a time, beating well after each addition, and adding a tablespoon of flour with the final egg to prevent curdling. Beat in the grated orange zest, then add the milk and fold in the remaining flour and baking powder. Very gently fold in the xantham gum (don't use any more than the stated amount otherwise your cake will be like chewing gum!); this is what stops the cake from crumbling. Don't overmix.

3. Now spoon the mixture into the tins, levelling them out and leaving a slight dip in the centre; this should help ensure the cakes stay level while baking. Bake for 20–25 minutes, until the tops spring back when pressed, if not, leave for a few more minutes. Once out of the oven, slide a knife round the outside of the tins to loosen and allow to cool in the tins completely, then transfer to a wire rack.

4. For the orange buttercream, beat the softened butter lightly until slightly paler in colour. Add half the icing sugar and stir in 2 tablespoons of the orange juice, then gently mix and add the remaining icing sugar and, if required, more juice.

5. Select the flattest cake for the top layer, pop the other one on the serving plate and spread half the buttercream over it. Don't spread it too close to the sides or it will seep out. Top with the second sponge then cover with the remaining buttercream. Use the Jelly Tots to decorate.

AUGUST

August
EDINBURGH TATTOO

ORANGE AND WHISKY LOAF

1st August
YORKSHIRE DAY

YORKSHIRE PARKIN

10th August
HENRY NESTLE'S
BIRTHDAY (1814)

WALNUT WHIP CAKE

15th August
INDIAN
INDEPENDENCE DAY

MASALA CHAI CAKE

16th August
PALIO DE SIENA

POLENTA AND
PISTACHIO CAKE

Late August
VENICE FILM FESTIVAL

ULTIMATE TIRAMISU CAKE

August Bank Holiday
NOTTING HILL CARNIVAL

GOLDEN PINEAPPLE
CREAM CAKE

Lynn Hill
Founder of
Clandestine Cake Club

The Royal Edinburgh Military Tattoo is an annual display of music, marching and military exercises held on the esplanade of Edinburgh Castle as part of the city's wider arts festival. Around 200,000 people join in a truly global gathering to enjoy the talents of international performers. Visitors to Scotland will no doubt want to stock up on a few home-grown treats, including their much-loved whisky and marmalade. But if you're looking for something a little more portable to take to the tattoo or the festival, a slice of this cake will keep spirits high and the castle chills at bay.

ORANGE AND WHISKY LOAF

SERVES 8–12

50g raisins

grated zest of 2 large oranges
(use the flesh in the syrup)

2 tbsp orange juice

230g self-raising wholemeal flour

230g unsalted butter, softened

230g soft light brown sugar

4 medium eggs, lightly beaten

SYRUP

2 tbsp marmalade
(any type you like)

2 tbsp soft light brown sugar

2 oranges, white pith removed,
separated into segments,
plus any residual juice

4 tbsp whisky

1 tbsp orange juice

1. Preheat the oven to 200°C/fan 180°C/gas 6. Grease and line a 900g loaf tin.

2. Place the raisins, orange zest and juice into a small bowl, mix together and leave to one side to infuse while you make the rest of the cake.

3. Sift the flour into a bowl, adding the wholemeal grains back into the flour from the sieve. Leave to one side.

4. In a separate bowl, beat the butter and sugar together with a wooden spoon or electric whisk, until light and creamy. Gradually add the eggs, beating well after each addition, and adding a tablespoon of the flour to help prevent curdling. Add the remaining flour and the orange-soaked raisins as well as their residual juice and zest. Mix until well combined.

5. Pour the batter into the tin and bake in the oven for 55–60 minutes or until a skewer inserted in the centre comes out clean. Leave in the tin to cool a little.

6. Make the syrup. Place the marmalade, sugar, orange segments and their residual juice, whisky and orange juice into a pan and heat gently until all the sugar has dissolved. Simmer for 10 minutes until you reach a syrupy consistency. Take off the heat and leave to cool for a few moments.

7. Pierce the cake with a skewer several times and brush the syrup over the cake while it is still in the tin. Arrange the syrupy orange segments down the centre, then pour over the remaining syrup. Leave to cool in the tin completely before turning out on to a wire rack or serving plate.

A Yorkshire parkin is only worthy of the Yorkshire name if it contains oatmeal (medium); anything less is just a ginger cake. So there is only one way to celebrate Yorkshire Day, when the county salutes its heritage. This is a cake that matures with age – the flavours develop and the crumb becomes even stickier so it is ideally made around two or three days before serving. Best accompanied with a strong cup of Yorkshire brew.

Lynn Hill
Founder of
Clandestine Cake Club

YORKSHIRE PARKIN

SERVES 14–16

200g unsalted butter

150g golden syrup

100g black treacle

100g soft dark brown sugar

110g medium oatmeal

180g self-raising flour

¾ tsp baking powder

1 tbsp ground ginger

2 large eggs, beaten

2 tbsp milk

1. Preheat the oven to 170°C/fan 150°C/gas 3. Grease and line a 20cm square tin with baking parchment.

2. Place the butter, golden syrup, treacle and brown sugar in a pan over a low heat. Gently simmer until all the sugar and butter have melted.

3. Place all the dry ingredients in a large heatproof bowl.

4. Pour the treacle mixture over the dry ingredients and mix until well combined. Add the beaten eggs gradually to avoid them scrambling in the hot mixture.

5. Pour into the tin and bake in the oven for 45–50 minutes or until a skewer inserted in the centre of the cake comes out clean. Do not open the oven until 40 minutes have passed otherwise the cake risks sinking. Cool in the tin for a few minutes before turning out on to a wire rack to cool completely. Parkin improves with age so you can keep it in an airtight container for at least a week before cutting.

Deborah Manger

Founded in 1866, Henry Nestlé's eponymous food and beverage company is now one of the largest in the world. Its stable includes many iconic brands and products, one of which is the Walnut Whip, a cone-shaped chocolate shell filled with a whipped vanilla fondant and topped with a walnut half. The Walnut Whip was launched in 1910 and, if the statistics are to be believed, remains as popular as ever: it is thought that in the UK somebody bites into one of these nutty chocolates every two seconds! Deborah has whipped the flavours of the iconic chocolate into a cake.

WALNUT WHIP CAKE

SERVES 12

6 medium eggs

180g caster sugar

180g plain flour

90g walnut oil

60g walnuts, coarsely chopped

CHOCOLATE GANACHE

150g good-quality dark chocolate (minimum 70 per cent cocoa solids), roughly broken

150ml double cream

BAVARIAN CREAM

4 gelatine leaves

250ml milk

85g caster sugar

35g cornflour

1 tsp vanilla extract

2 large egg yolks

250ml double cream

100g toasted, chopped walnuts, blitzed to a paste

1. Start by making the ganache. Place the chocolate and cream in a heatproof bowl set over a pan of simmering water and allow to melt. Remove the bowl and leave to cool at room temperature for about 1–2 hours, until it has spreading consistency.

2. Preheat the oven to 180°C/fan 160°C/gas 4. Grease and line two 20cm cake tins.

3. Whisk the eggs and sugar until the whisk leaves a 'ribbon trail' when lifted from the mixture. Fold in half the flour and half the oil, then fold in the remaining half of each. Gently stir in the chopped walnuts. Divide the cake mixture between the cake tins, leaving 1cm free at the top (you may have a little more mixture than you need but it's important to leave this gap.

4. Bake for 20–25 minutes until golden and firm to the touch. Remove from the oven and cool in the tins for 10 minutes before turning out on to wire racks to cool completely.

5. Make the Bavarian cream. Soak the gelatine in cold water for 10 minutes. Heat the milk and sugar in a medium saucepan until almost boiling.

6. Whisk the cornflour, vanilla and egg yolks together, then gradually whisk in the sweetened milk. Return the mixture to the pan and continue heating and stirring until thickened.

7. Drain the gelatine and stir it into the warm custard until fully dissolved, then remove from the heat. Whip the cream until stiff. Stir the walnut paste into the warm custard, then fold in the whipped cream. Cover the surface with cling film to prevent a skin forming.

MARSHMALLOW

3 gelatine leaves

1 large egg white

225g caster sugar

½ tbsp glucose syrup

½ tsp vanilla extract

100ml water

DECORATION

12 walnut halves

50g walnuts, chopped

8. Make the marshmallow. Soak the gelatine in cold water for 10 minutes. Whip the egg white until soft peaks form.

9. Heat the sugar, glucose syrup, vanilla extract and water until a thermometer reaches 127°C and the sugar has dissolved. Remove the gelatine from its liquid and add it to the syrup without squeezing out the water. Pour the syrup mixture into the egg white while whisking constantly, but be very careful to pour the syrup down the sides of the bowl away from the whisk to prevent scalding hot syrup flying everywhere. Continue whisking until the mixture holds stiff peaks.

10. To assemble, slice each sponge into two layers. Spread a layer of cream between three of the layers, leaving the top layer clean. Cover the top and sides with the marshmallow and leave to set in the fridge for 1 hour.

11. Cover the outside of the cake with the ganache. Decorate the top with the walnut halves and chopped walnuts.

Beckey Barton

The Venice Film Festival is the oldest film festival in the world. It forms part of the 'biennale', a dizzying cultural carnival that celebrates the arts. There's so much to see and do at the festival that spectators might be in need of a 'tiramisù' (literally a 'pick-me-up'). Tiramisù is an Italian dessert made of sponge cakes soaked in coffee and liqueur, then layered with a sweet, thick custard. Beckey's cake takes all the flavours of the popular pudding and piles them into a cake soaked in a Marsala wine syrup and topped with a mascarpone cream frosting.

ULTIMATE TIRAMISU CAKE

SERVES 12

25ml strong black coffee

100ml milk

½ tsp vanilla extract

225g unsalted butter, softened

105g demerara sugar

120g dark muscovado sugar

175g self-raising flour

100g plain flour

½ tsp baking powder

4 medium eggs, lightly beaten

SOAKING SYRUP

2 tbsp Marsala wine

40ml hot water

few drops of cappuccino extract

70g caster sugar

FROSTING

150ml double cream

60g unsalted butter, softened

125g mascarpone

350g icing sugar

few drops of custard flavouring

cocoa powder, to decorate

1. Preheat the oven to 180°C/fan 160°C/gas 4. Line the base of two 20cm sandwich tins with baking parchment, then grease the sides of the tin and lightly dust with flour.

2. Combine the coffee, milk and vanilla extract and set aside. Using an electric whisk, beat the butter and both sugars until creamy. In a separate bowl, sift together both flours with the baking powder and set aside.

3. With the whisk running at a low speed, slowly add the eggs to the butter and sugar mixture with a tablespoon of flour to prevent curdling.

4. Stop the whisk and, using a wooden spoon, mix in a third of the milk and coffee mixture, then a third of the flour. When fully combined repeat the process until all of the coffee, milk and flour are mixed in.

5. Divide the mixture between the two tins and bake for 25–30 minutes until they spring back when pressed.

6. While the cakes are in the oven make the soaking syrup by putting all of the ingredients in a small saucepan and bringing to a simmer. Stir gently over a medium heat for 5 minutes until reduced slightly.

7. As soon as the cakes come out of the oven, brush the tops liberally with the warm syrup then leave to cool completely in the tins. Meanwhile, make the frosting.

8. Whip the double cream in a bowl until it forms soft peaks, then set aside. Beat the butter and mascarpone, then gradually add the icing sugar until everything is combined. If the mixture is too dry, add a little of the whipped cream to soften. Once the frosting is smooth, add the custard flavouring and then carefully fold in the whipped cream.

9. To assemble, sandwich the two cakes with a thin layer of the frosting, then spread it liberally over the top. When ready to serve, sprinkle a generous coating of cocoa powder on the top. This cake is best kept in the fridge for up to 3 days because of the cream and mascarpone in the frosting.

Indian Independence Day celebrates the anniversary of when the country gained its independence from the British Empire in 1947. As one of the world's largest producers of tea, India is unquestionably a nation of tea drinkers, and the most widely consumed is 'masala chai', a sweet milky tea flavoured with spices and herbs. Deepa has used cardamom, cloves, ginger and black pepper as the basis of her warming masala mix but the spices can vary according to the cook. The chai blend is used to infuse a tea syrup, which then laces both the sponge and the buttercream of this fragrant cake. Why not serve with glasses of milky chai?

Deepa Mistry

MASALA CHAI CAKE

SERVES 10–12

250g unsalted butter, softened

100g soft dark brown sugar

150g caster sugar

1 tsp masala chai syrup
(see below)

4 large eggs

250g self-raising flour

40–50g unsalted pistachios,
roughly chopped, to decorate

MASALA CHAI

2 cardamom pods, seeds only

1 clove

1 tsp ground ginger

½ tsp black pepper

MASALA CHAI SYRUP

120g caster sugar

100ml very strongly brewed
black tea

4 tsp masala chai (see above,
or use shop-bought)

> *Ingredients and recipe
continue overleaf*

1. Start by preparing the masala chai. Grind all the ingredients in a spice grinder or with a pestle and mortar, to form a powder.

2. Next make the syrup. Place all the ingredients in a small saucepan and bring to the boil, stirring all the time. Reduce the heat to medium and simmer until the syrup thickens enough just to coat the back of a spoon. Keep stirring often with a spatula so it doesn't stick and make sure you stay with the syrup at all times – it can burn very quickly. Once ready, leave it in the saucepan until you are ready to use it for your cake.

3. Preheat the oven to 200°C/fan 180°C/gas 6. Grease and line two 20cm loose-bottomed cake tins.

4. Beat the butter and sugars using a wooden spoon or electric whisk, until light and fluffy. Add the masala chai syrup then add the eggs one at a time, beating well after each addition, and adding a tablespoon of the flour with each egg to help prevent curdling. Add the remaining flour in thirds, folding it in carefully or mixing slowly with the whisk. Divide the mixture equally between the tins.

5. Bake for 20–25 minutes or until a skewer inserted in the centre of the cakes comes out clean. Leave to cool in the tins for 15 minutes, then remove and place upside down on a wire rack. Pour around half of the syrup over each cake, then leave it to soak in as the cakes cool. Make sure the rest of the syrup is cool before you make the buttercream. ❯

CHAI BUTTERCREAM

400g icing sugar

pinch of salt

235g unsalted butter, softened

1 tbsp masala chai syrup

6. For the buttercream, beat the sugar, salt and butter until smooth and light. Gently fold in the cooled tablespoon of syrup and set aside till ready to use.

7. To assemble, arrange one cake half on a plate or cake stand, pipe or spread the buttercream on to the cake. Drizzle over any remaining syrup and then sandwich with your other cake. Pipe or spread more buttercream on top. Scatter the chopped pistachios over the top, and drizzle on more syrup, if you wish. The cake can be stored in a cake tin in a cool place for 2 days.

Note

Masala chai can be bought in most Asian supermarkets, or online via specialist Indian grocers. It is easy to make a small or large batch yourself, and it keeps in a jar, stored in a cool, dark place, for around three months.

'Il Palio', as it is known locally, is a horserace held twice a year in Siena in Italy. Ten jockeys ride bareback around the Piazza del Campo three times and, although the race itself usually lasts no more than 90 seconds, it is preceded by a celebratory pageant. Yasmine's tribute to the festivities takes its inspiration from the northern-Italian peasant dish, polenta, which is made by boiling up cornmeal. The rich nutty flavour of pistachios complements the slightly sweet cornmeal in this wonderfully moist and dense cake.

Yasmine Tamer

POLENTA AND PISTACHIO CAKE

SERVES 8–10

150g unsalted butter, at room temperature, plus extra for greasing

50ml vegetable oil

200g light muscovado sugar

200g shelled pistachios, plus extra for topping

100g fine cornmeal

pinch of salt

1 tsp baking powder

3 medium eggs, beaten

grated zest of 2 lemons

1. Preheat the oven to 180°C/160°C fan/gas 4. Line the base of a 20cm springform cake tin with baking parchment and grease the sides.

2. Beat the butter, oil and sugar until pale and fluffy. Using a food processor or hand blender, grind the pistachios as finely as desired (be careful not to overgrind as this will make a paste).

3. Mix together the ground pistachios, cornmeal, salt and baking powder. While still beating, pour one third of the pistachio mix into the butter mix, followed by half the beaten eggs. Repeat this process with another third of the pistachio mix, the rest of the eggs, then the last third of the pistachio mix. Lastly, stir in the lemon zest.

4. Pour the mixture into the prepared tin, scatter with the extra pistachios and bake in the oven for 45–55 minutes or until a skewer inserted in the centre of the cake comes out clean. Remove from the oven and leave to cool in the tin placed on a wire rack. Some sinking in thé cake is normal with such a dense batter. The cake will stay moist for 5–6 days in an airtight tin.

Nikki Dennis

As street festivals go, Notting Hill Carnival must be the biggest and most colourful in Europe. It began in 1964 as a way of bringing together Afro-Caribbean communities to celebrate their cultures and traditions, and every year the streets of West London come alive with music, dancing and the wonderful aroma of traditional Caribbean food. This vibrant pineapple cake is every bit as lively as the celebrations and will bring a bit of sunshine to your table as you slice into the tropical sponge.

GOLDEN PINEAPPLE CREAM CAKE

SERVES 10–12

1 small pineapple

4 large eggs

400g caster sugar

1 tsp vanilla extract

240g plain flour

2 tsp baking powder

¼ tsp salt

120ml milk

60g unsalted butter

120ml shop-bought pineapple juice

PINEAPPLE BUTTERCREAM

240g unsalted butter, softened

400g icing sugar

1 tbsp vanilla extract

2 tbsp double cream

2 tbsp pineapple juice

yellow gel food colouring

1. Preheat the oven to 190°C/fan 170°C/gas 5. Grease and line two 22cm cake tins.

2. Cut the skin off pineapple and remove the core. Dice the pineapple finely, then set aside.

3. Beat the eggs with an electric whisk for 4 minutes. Add the sugar and continue beating for another 4–5 minutes, until light and fluffy. Add the vanilla and stir until just combined.

4. Combine the flour, baking powder and salt in a bowl. Add to the egg mixture on a low speed.

5. Place the milk, butter and pineapple juice in a small saucepan and heat until the butter has melted, then add to the batter mixture. Mix in 60g of the diced pineapple, then pour the batter into the tins.

6. Bake for 25–30 minutes or until a skewer inserted into the centre of the cake comes out clean. Remove from the oven and allow to cool in the tins for at least 10 minutes, then turn out on to a wire rack to cool completely.

7. For the buttercream, beat the butter with an electric whisk, until creamy. Add the icing sugar and continue to beat on a low speed until combined. Add the vanilla, cream and pineapple juice and beat on a high speed for 3 minutes. Add more icing sugar or pineapple juice to achieve the desired consistency, than add the food colouring.

8. Remove a third of the buttercream to a separate bowl and add 60g of the diced pineapple. Spread this over the bottom layer of the cake. Top with the second cake. Using a palette knife, cover the whole cake with a very thin layer of frosting – a 'crumb coat'. Chill for 20–30 minutes, then cover the whole cake with the remaining buttercream. This cake needs to be stored in the fridge and eaten within 1–2 days.

SEPTEMBER

September

JEWISH NEW YEAR

APPLE AND HONEY CAKE

3rd September

DUCHESS OF BEDFORD'S
BIRTHDAY (1783)

PEAR AND GINGER
UPSIDE-DOWN CAKE

Early September

LAST NIGHT
OF THE PROMS

OPERA CAKE

16th September

FIRST BRITISH ASSEMBLY
OF THE
WOMEN'S INSTITUTE
(1915)

VICTORIA SANDWICH

Late September

HARVEST FESTIVAL

CAKE OF GOODNESS

21st September

INTERNATIONAL
PEACE DAY

OLIVE OIL, ROSEMARY
AND LIME WREATH

29th September

MICHAELMAS DAY

BEETROOT AND APPLE CAKE

Lynn Hill
Founder of
Clandestine Cake Club

Rosh Hashanah (meaning 'Head of the Year') is the celebration of the Jewish New Year. It is the first of the High Holy Days, a 10-day celebration ending with the holiest date in the Jewish calendar, Yom Kippur, a fasting holiday. There are many symbolic foods associated with Rosh Hashanah, all eaten in the hope of enjoying a promising year. It is customary to avoid sour or tart flavours, while sweet foods are consumed in abundance. Honey is considered particularly auspicious. It's traditional to enjoy apples dipped in sweet honey before the meal on the night of Rosh Hashanah, while a moist honey cake often completes the feast. Aromatic spices and strong black coffee add warmth and depth to this generous apple and honey cake, a suitably sweet way to bring in an abundant and happy new year.

APPLE AND HONEY CAKE

SERVES 12–14

300g self-raising flour

1 tsp ground cinnamon

¼ tsp mixed spice

½ tsp baking powder

pinch of salt

2 medium eggs

100g light brown sugar

100g dark brown sugar

125ml vegetable oil

200g honey (runny or set)

125ml warm, freshly brewed, strong black coffee

2 medium eating apples, peeled, cored and grated

30g raisins or sultanas

25g flaked almonds

icing sugar, to dust

1. Preheat the oven to 200°C/fan 180°C/gas 6. Grease and line a 23cm springform cake tin.

2. Sift the flour, spices, baking powder and salt together and leave to one side.

3. In a separate bowl, beat the eggs and sugars together until light and creamy. In a jug, mix the oil, honey and coffee. Add to the egg batter and mix until well combined.

4. Gradually add the flour mixture to the wet ingredients giving it a good mix and making sure there are no lumps of flour and that everything is well combined. Add the apple and give it a good mix, then add the raisins and flaked almonds and stir until well combined.

5. Pour the batter into the tin and bake for 40–45 minutes or until a skewer inserted in the centre of the cake comes out clean. You may need to cover the cake with foil for the last 10–15 minutes if it looks as though it is browning too quickly. Leave in the tin to cool for around 15 minutes before turning out on to a wire rack to cool completely. Dust with icing sugar before serving.

Anna Maria Russell, the seventh Duchess of Bedford, is widely regarded as the creator of the English afternoon tea. The duchess is believed to have described a certain mid-afternoon 'sinking feeling' (dinner was usually served very late in the day), so asked her maid to bring her a tray of tea, bread, butter and small cakes in her private boudoir to tide her over until the evening. The practice became well established after she invited friends to join her. Today, a traditional afternoon tea can be a grand affair, compared with the light meal once intended, with its finger sandwiches, tea, scones and cakes of every kind. Afternoon hunger pangs can certainly be kept at bay with this fruity cream-filled cake. It's simple enough to give a nod to the meal's modest origins, yet indulgent enough to feel like a true celebration of what has become a great British tradition.

Jean Lacey

PEAR AND GINGER UPSIDE-DOWN CAKE

SERVES 6–8

200g self-raising flour

1 tsp baking powder

1 tsp ground ginger

200g golden caster sugar

200g unsalted butter, softened

4 large eggs

2 tbsp milk

TOPPING

75g soft light brown sugar

2 ripe pears

FILLING

125ml double cream

1 tbsp icing sugar

2 tbsp ginger preserve

1. Preheat the oven to 180°C/fan 160°C/gas 4. Grease two 20cm sandwich tins, line the sides and bases with baking parchment and grease again.

2. Sift the flour, baking powder and ginger into a large bowl. Add all the other cake ingredients and beat with an electric whisk until fully combined and smooth.

3. To prepare the topping, sprinkle the soft brown sugar evenly over the bottom of one of the tins.

4. Peel the pears, halve them, remove the cores and slice each half into three wedges. Arrange the pear slices on top of the brown sugar.

5. Divide the cake mixture evenly between the two tins, being careful not to disturb the pear slices and remembering that the tin with the fruit on the bottom will inevitably look fuller. Bake for 20–25 minutes or until a skewer inserted in the centre of the cakes comes out clean. The one with the pears on the bottom will take about 5 minutes longer than the other. Leave to cool in the tins for 5–10 minutes, then carefully turn out on to a wire rack to cool completely.

6. For the filling, whip the double cream with the icing sugar until thick enough to be spreadable.

7. When the cakes are cold, spread the preserve over the plain cake layer (warm it slightly in a small pan if necessary to make it runny enough to spread, but then allow it to cool completely before letting it touch any cream). Spread a thick layer of whipped cream on top, then cover with the fruited cake (fruit-side up)

The word 'prom' is short for 'promenade concert', a term dating back to the eighteenth century when outdoor concerts were held in London's pleasure gardens and the audience was free to stroll around while the orchestra played. These days, the Proms are an eight-week summer season of daily orchestral performances and other events, which culminate in the Last Night of the Proms. Held at the Royal Albert Hall, the final event is lighter and in many ways different from other prom nights in that the music includes popular classics and patriotic British numbers as well as choral pieces and even the odd singalong. The finale to such a magnificent musical display demands a celebration to match. So why not bake one of the grandest cakes named after a performing art? With its layers of cream, liqueur-soaked sponge and chocolate ganache, this refined and elegant opera cake is the perfect encore.

Lynn Hill
Founder of
Clandestine Cake Club

OPERA CAKE

SERVES 8–10

3 large egg whites

20g caster sugar

110g ground almonds

110g icing sugar

3 large eggs

35g plain flour, sifted

35g unsalted butter, melted

4 tbsp liqueur of your choice

CRÈME LEGÈRE

2 large eggs

60g caster sugar

30g plain flour or cornflour

300ml double cream

1 vanilla pod, seeds scraped

60g unsalted butter

❯ *Ingredients and recipe continue overleaf*

1. Grease and line a 35 x 25cm Swiss roll tin with baking parchment.

2. Using an electric whisk, whisk the egg whites in a bowl until you have stiff peaks. Gradually add the sugar, beating all the time, until all the sugar has dissolved and you have a shiny meringue. Set aside.

3. Beat together the ground almonds, icing sugar and whole eggs until the mixture has doubled in size –this will take about 4 minutes. Fold in the flour, then carefully fold in the meringue mixture in stages taking care not to lose all those lovely air bubbles. Finally incorporate the melted butter by pouring it down the side of the bowl and folding in.

4. Pour the mixture into the Swiss roll tin, taking care to level it out. Bake in the oven for 9–12 minutes or until a light golden brown. Remove from the oven and invert on to a clean sheet of baking parchment. Peel away the backing paper but leave it covering the sponge. Leave to cool completely.

5. Make the crème legère. In a heatproof bowl, beat together the eggs, sugar and flour until well combined.

6. Gently heat 200ml of the cream with the vanilla pod and seeds until bubbles appear on the surface. Pass through a sieve before pouring over the egg mixture and mixing until well combined.

7. Return the mixture to a clean pan and gently heat, beating all the time to avoid lumps forming. As soon as the mixture thickens, take it off the heat and add the butter, beating until melted and incorporated. Cover the surface of the crème with cling film to prevent a skin forming and leave to one side to cool completely.

8. Whip the remaining cream until the whisk leaves a ribbon trail when lifted, then add to the cold crème. Beat until light and smooth. Leave in the fridge until required. ❯

CHOCOLATE GANACHE

100ml double cream

100ml dark chocolate
(70 per cent cocoa solids),
chopped into small pieces

1 tsp liqueur of your choice

TO FINISH

100g caster sugar

24 whole blanched almonds,
plus 100g, chopped

9. Make the ganache. Place the chocolate in a heatproof bowl. Gently heat the cream until bubbles appear on the side of the pan. Pour the cream over the chocolate and leave to infuse for 2 minutes. Do not stir. Pour in the liqueur, then starting at the centre, begin to stir and incorporate the whole mixture together. Set aside until cool, then transfer to the fridge to chill.

10. Meanwhile, prepare the caramelised almonds for the topping. Put the sugar into a small saucepan over a low heat and leave it to melt and start to turn golden. At this point, add the almonds, swirl the pan then stir the nuts with metal fork (not a wooden spoon) to turn them and make sure they are coated. Turn off the heat, lift the nuts out with the fork and place on a wire rack set over a baking tray to cool.

11. To assemble the cake, cut the sponge into four equal layers, then slice two of these layers in half horizontally to make six in total. Drizzle your chosen liqueur over each sponge. Leave for a few moments to soak in.

12. Place one of the thicker layers on to a cake stand or plate and spread with one third of the chocolate ganache. Place one of the thin sponge layers on top then cover this with about a third of the crème legère. Place another of the thin sponge layers on top and spread with the second third of ganache.

13. Repeat these two thin layers, then top with the remaining thick sponge layer. For neat sides place the cake in the fridge for about 15 minutes to firm up a little, then take a large sharp knife and square off all four edges. Spread the remaining crème legère over the top and sides of the cake, then press the chopped almonds over the whole cake and decorate the top with the caramelised almonds. Chill if not serving immediately.

Although the first Women's Institute (WI) was founded in Ontario, Canada, in 1897, it didn't arrive in Britain until September 1915, when it was formed to encourage women to help their war-torn nation by growing and preserving food. The aims of the organisation have since expanded and it now provides women with educational opportunities as well as the chance to develop and learn new skills. The WI is synonymous with exacting standards, most famously when it comes to baking cakes and making preserves. This classic Victoria sandwich, perhaps the most iconic of British cakes, and certainly an extremely precise one, is the perfect tribute to the knowledge and skills of such an esteemed and treasured organisation.

Lynn Hill
Founder of
Clandestine Cake Club

VICTORIA SANDWICH

SERVES 8–10

225g unsalted butter, softened

225g caster sugar, plus a little extra to dust

4 medium eggs, lightly beaten

1 tsp vanilla paste

225g self-raising flour

1 tbsp milk

FILLING

4 tbsp good-quality seedless raspberry jam

1. Preheat the oven to 200°C/fan 180°C/gas 6. Grease and line the base of two loose-bottomed 20cm sandwich tins.

2. Beat the butter and sugar using a wooden spoon or electric whisk, until light and fluffy. Gradually add the egg and vanilla paste, beating well after each addition, and adding a tablespoon of flour with the final bit of egg to help prevent curdling. Fold in the remaining flour until well combined, then mix in the milk.

3. Pour the mixture into the cake tins, levelling the surface, and bake for 20–25 minutes or until a skewer inserted in the centre of the cakes come out clean. Leave in the tins for 5 minutes to cool a little before turning out on to a wire rack to cool completely.

4. Sandwich the layers together with the raspberry jam and dust the top with caster sugar. Classic.

Deborah Tidder

Harvest festivals are celebrated around the world at different times of the year according to the nation's main harvest. The festival is a celebration of thanks for the year's crops and a time of sharing gifts, and in Britain it is most commonly observed in churches and schools where donations are collected to be given to those in need. So why not bake your own contribution and celebrate the season's beautiful sweet root vegetables by offering them up to share in a slice of cake.

CAKE OF GOODNESS

SERVES 8–10

250g wholemeal flour, sifted

250g self-raising flour, sifted

250g soft light brown sugar

2 tsp salt

½ tsp ground ginger

½ tsp ground nutmeg

1 tsp ground cinnamon

4 large eggs

200ml sunflower oil

100g desiccated coconut

150g sultanas

100g sunflower seeds

100g pumpkin seeds

50g each of peeled sweet potato, beetroot and parsnip, grated

100g peeled carrot, grated

TOPPING

75g soft margarine or unsalted butter, softened

30g cream cheese

300g icing sugar, plus 1 tsp

grated zest of 2 oranges

handful of pumpkin and sunflower seeds

1. Preheat the oven to 190°C/fan 170°C/gas 5. Grease and line a 20cm cake tin or 900g loaf tin.

2. Mix together the flours, sugar, salt and spices, then add the eggs and oil. Stir until well combined, then add the rest of the ingredients. Mix thoroughly then pour into the tin and bake in the centre of the oven for 1–1½ hours (keep checking it after the first hour). The cake is ready when a skewer inserted in the centre comes out clean. Leave to cool in the tin for 15 minutes, then turn out on to a wire rack to cool completely while you make the topping.

3. Whisk the margarine and cream cheese, then add the icing sugar and orange zest and continue to whisk until you have a piping consistency.

4. Once the cake is cool, pipe on the topping, then mix the seeds with a teaspoon of icing sugar and sprinkle over the top.

Note

Without its topping, the cake freezes well.

Lynn Hill
Founder of
Clandestine Cake Club

In 1982, the United Nations General Assembly launched an International Day of Peace as a way of inviting the world to cease hostilities and to celebrate peaceful initiatives. Every year, the Secretary General inaugurates the day with a speech and by ringing the United Nations peace bell. Olive branches have long been recognised as a symbol of peace, while since the Middle Ages, rosemary has been worn by brides, grooms and guests at wedding ceremonies, linking it to love and happiness. So, in order to celebrate 'peace and love' on this important day, here is a delicate, light sponge made with rosemary-infused olive oil, baked in the shape of a wreath and topped with a simple white glacé icing.

OLIVE OIL, ROSEMARY AND LIME WREATH

SERVES 10–12

cake release spray, for the tin

170ml extra virgin olive oil

grated zest of 2 limes and the juice of 1

2 tbsp chopped rosemary

200g caster sugar

4 medium eggs

140ml milk

400g self-raising flour

½ tsp fine sea salt

GLACÉ ICING

100g icing sugar, sifted

1–2 tbsp cooled boiled water

rosemary sprigs, to decorate (optional)

1. Preheat the oven to 190°C/fan 170°C/gas 5. Spray a 25cm fluted cake ring tin with cake release spray.

2. Place the olive oil in a measuring jug. Add the lime zest and juice and rosemary and leave to infuse while you make the rest of the cake.

3. Using an electric whisk, beat the sugar and eggs together until tripled in volume. It should look nice and creamy, like whipped double cream, but still be slightly runny. This should take only about 5 minutes.

4. While still beating, add the olive oil mixture to the egg mixture and continue to beat until well combined. Beat in the milk. Gradually add the flour and salt and beat until well combined.

5. Pour the mixture into the tin and bake in the oven for 40–45 minutes or until a skewer inserted in the centre of the cake comes out clean. Leave in the tin to cool completely, then ease out of the tin.

6. Make the icing by mixing the icing sugar and water together until you have a thick runny consistency. Drizzle over the cake, then decorate with rosemary sprigs, if you wish.

Michaelmas is celebrated on the 29th September every year. As it falls just after the equinox, it is often associated with the shortening of days and the beginning of autumn. So why not celebrate the abundance of seasonal fruit and vegetables available at this time of year by baking this bountiful cake? The deep red of beetroot juice naturally tints the striking cream topping of this cake while the grated flesh gives the sponge a wonderful earthy texture, flavour and moistness. And to embrace autumn's harvest further still, this cake gives a nod to the diversity of British apples by offsetting the sweet, crisp Cox's Orange Pippins in the sponge with a tart Bramley purée to sandwich the cake. (Pictured overleaf.)

Mike Wallis

BEETROOT AND APPLE CAKE

SERVES 8

juice of 1 lemon

1 tbsp icing sugar

1 medium beetroot, peeled and grated

1 Cox's Orange Pippin apple, peeled and grated

120g unsalted butter, softened

120g light muscovado sugar

2 large eggs

140g self-raising flour

½ tsp baking powder

1 tbsp icing sugar

125ml whipping cream

APPLE PURÉE

1 Bramley apple, peeled, cored and cut into chunks

1 tbsp caster sugar

pinch of ground cinnamon

1 tsp butter

1. Make the apple purée. Put the Bramley apple, sugar and cinnamon in a small saucepan and cook over a gentle heat until the apples have broken down completely and are very smooth when beaten. Take off the heat and beat in the butter. Leave to cool completely.

2. Preheat the oven to 200°C/fan 180°C/gas 6. Grease and line a 20cm cake tin.

3. Mix the lemon juice and icing sugar together, then add the beetroot and apple. Leave to infuse and macerate for at least 20 minutes.

4. Beat the butter and sugar using a wooden spoon or electric whisk, until light and fluffy. Add the eggs one at a time, beating well after each addition. Drain the grated beetroot and apple (reserving the liquid), and fold into the mixture. Sift the flour and baking powder into the mixture, a third at a time and fold in until just combined. The mixture will be very pink.

5. Pour into the tin and bake for 50 minutes or until a skewer inserted in the centre of the cake comes out clean. Leave in the tin for a few minutes to cool, then transfer to a wire rack to cool completely. You'll notice that after baking the cake doesn't look quite so pink, but the beetroot gives it bright red speckles.

6. Mix the icing sugar with the cream and whip to soft peaks. Fold in a tablespoon of the reserved macerating liquid (or more, if you would like a deeper colour).

7. Slice the cake in half and spread the apple purée on one half, then spread half the cream mixture onto the other layer and sandwich the two together. Top the cake with the remaining cream mixture.

OCTOBER

1st October
WALT DISNEY WORLD
FLORIDA OPENED (1971)

CHOCOLATE KEY LIME CAKE

2nd October
MAHATMA GANDHI'S
BIRTHDAY (1869)

RASPBERRY AND
ASSAM TEA LOAF

5th October
WORLD TEACHERS' DAY

TOFFEE APPLE GINGERBREAD

10th October
WORLD MENTAL
HEALTH DAY

CHOCOLATE ORANGE CAKE

Mid to late October
APPLE DAY

TAFFETY CAKE

Late October
DIWALI

PISTACHIO AND COCONUT
BARFI CAKE

31st October
HALLOWE'EN

SPICED PUMPKIN CAKE

Claire Howarth

Born in India in 1869, Mohandas Karamchand Gandhi was the leader of the Indian nationalist movement against British rule and is widely considered one of the greatest political and spiritual leaders the world has ever seen. Known as 'Mahatma', meaning 'great soul', Gandhi is renowned for his non-violent demonstrations and inspiring struggle for justice. To celebrate the life of such a remarkable man, this fragrant, moist loaf cake is made with one of his nation's biggest exports, tea. The malty notes of Assam tea are a lovely complement to tart raspberries but you could try using a Darjeeling if you like, which would also be a natural partner to the gentle warmth of cinnamon.

RASPBERRY AND ASSAM TEA LOAF

SERVES 10

150ml semi-skimmed milk

2 Assam or Darjeeling teabags

200g caster sugar

2 medium eggs

½ tsp vanilla extract

200g plain flour, sifted

1 heaped tsp baking powder

1 tsp ground cinnamon

75ml vegetable oil

120g raspberries

FROSTING

70g margarine or unsalted butter, softened

130g icing sugar

3 raspberries

1. Preheat the oven to 190°C/fan 170°C/gas 5. Grease and line a 900g loaf tin.

2. Bring the milk to the boil then drop in the teabags. Stir then remove from the heat and put to one side (with the teabags still in the milk) and leave it to steep as it cools.

3. Beat the sugar, eggs and vanilla extract using an electric whisk on a medium–high speed until thoroughly combined and the mixture resembles a thick paste.

4. Add the flour, baking powder, cinnamon, vegetable oil and 100ml of the tea-flavoured milk (you will find the teabags absorb some of the milk so you will probably need to give them a squeeze to get your 100ml out of the original 150ml). Mix on a slow speed until fully incorporated – take care not to overmix.

5. In a separate bowl, gently crush the raspberries (a potato masher works). You want them to retain their size and rough shape but just start to release their juice. Add the raspberries to the cake mix and stir them in by hand.

6. Pour the mixture into the loaf tin and bake for 45–50 minutes or until a skewer inserted in the centre of the cake comes out clean. Leave to cool in the tin for 10 minutes then turn out on to a wire rack to cool completely.

7. While the cake is baking you can make the frosting. Place the margarine or butter in a large bowl and sift the icing sugar over the top. Cream the ingredients together. Press the raspberries through a sieve to give a purée (and remove the seeds). Gradually add the purée to the frosting mix, stirring gently. You may not need to add all the purée and take care not to overmix or it might start to separate (it will still taste nice but will not look as pretty). Once the cake is cool, spread the frosting over the top.

Yin Li

Created by UNESCO in 1994, World Teachers' Day raises awareness of the essential role that teachers play in the education of future generations and rallies for support to ensure that everyone around the world has access to quality schooling. With the important work that teachers do, it's only natural that students want to say thank you by giving them gifts. While offering a teacher an apple might be the traditional approach, why not go one step further by baking this sticky, sweet toffee apple cake instead?

TOFFEE APPLE GINGERBREAD

SERVES 10–12

225g self-raising flour

1 tsp bicarbonate of soda

1½ tbsp ground ginger

1 tsp ground cinnamon

1 tsp mixed spice

115g unsalted butter,
from the fridge,
cut into small cubes

115g black treacle

115g golden syrup

115g dark brown
muscovado sugar

275ml milk

1 large egg, lightly beaten

1. Preheat the oven to 180°C/fan 160°C/gas 4. Grease and line the base and sides of a square 20cm tin with a single piece of baking paper so that the tin is sealed and the toffee can't escape.

2. For the toffee apples, in a large frying pan, melt the butter and sugar together over a medium heat until the mixture starts to go brown and bubble, then add the apples to the pan. Do be careful because the juiciness of the apples may cause the sugar mixture to splutter and sizzle slightly but hold your nerve because if you mix gently to coat the apples in it, it will come together again. Cook for about 5 minutes until the apples are nice and glossy, and just starting to soften. They don't need to be completely cooked because they will be cooked further. Remove from the heat and allow to cool.

3. Line the base of the tin with the apples. You will probably have quite a lot of sauce, but pour in as much as you like to make a stickier apple layer.

4. Sift the flour, bicarbonate of soda and all the spices together into a large bowl to ensure they are well mixed with no lumps. Add the cubes of butter to the bowl and use your fingertips to rub them into the mixture, until the texture is like breadcrumbs. Set to one side.

5. Place the treacle and golden syrup in a pan on a low heat and warm until melted and runny, not hot and bubbling. Put to one side so that it cools to lukewarm.

TOFFEE APPLES

100g unsalted butter

100g golden caster sugar

6 Granny Smith apples or other sharp, crisp eating apples, peeled, cored, each apple cut into 6 wedges

6. Place the sugar and the milk in a small saucepan over a low heat and allow the sugar to dissolve. Note that muscovado sugar can form little lumps so make sure these are broken up with a fork or small whisk to ensure they dissolve fully, then let the mixture cool to lukewarm.

7. For the final stage, you need to work quickly because the liquid will activate the bicarbonate of soda. Firstly, whisk the milk mixture into the flour mixture and beat well, then beat in the treacle mixture followed by the egg. You're aiming for a smooth, thick and well-blended batter, which will start to look quite bubbly. Pour it over the apple layer in the tin.

8. Bake in the oven for 50–60 minutes or until a skewer inserted in the centre of the cake comes out clean. Allow to cool completely in the tin before removing.

9. You can either serve the cake with the caramelised apple layer on top – reminiscent of a tarte Tatin – or you may prefer to leave the apples on the base so that it is a surprise at the bottom. Also, like any gingerbread, this cake improves with keeping, so once cold, wrap in foil and try to resist for a day or two so that it becomes even stickier.

Fiona O'Donnell

Members have often said how joining the Clandestine Cake Club has made their lives so much richer (beyond the butter and sugar!), and some say that baking has helped them through difficult times in their lives. Focusing on baking for a few hours can transport you away from troubling thoughts and offer you a creative outlet. World Mental Health Day is held annually to raise awareness of mental health and to focus on making mental-health care a reality for people around the world. Why not spend a few hours baking this easy, zingy chocolate cake with friends? Not only is the combination of endorphin-packed chocolate and zesty orange a nice boost, you will also have the uplifting satisfaction of sharing your creation with others and seeing their enjoyment as they get stuck in.

CHOCOLATE ORANGE CAKE

SERVES 12–14

225g self-raising flour

1½ tsp baking powder

225g caster sugar

225g unsalted butter, softened

4 medium eggs

grated zest of 1 orange,
plus 1 tbsp juice

1 tbsp cocoa powder

CHOCOLATE ORANGE ICING

150g icing sugar

1 tbsp cocoa powder

3 tbsp freshly-squeezed
orange juice

1. Preheat the oven to 180°C/fan 160°C/gas 4. Grease and line a 23cm springform cake tin.

2. Sift the flour and baking powder into a large bowl. Add the sugar, butter and eggs and beat until pale and creamy. Divide the mixture evenly between two bowls.

3. Add the orange zest and juice to one half of the cake mixture and stir gently until combined.

4. Dissolve the cocoa powder in 2 tablespoons of hot water, then add to the second half of the cake mixture and stir gently until combined.

5. Spoon the mixtures randomly into the prepared baking tin then swirl with a knife for a marbled effect. Bake in the oven for 35–45 minutes or until a skewer inserted in the centre of the cake comes out clean. Leave to cool in the tin for 10 minutes then turn out on to a wire rack to cool completely.

6. To prepare the icing, sift the icing sugar and cocoa powder into a bowl, then add the orange juice a tablespoon at a time and stir until the mixture reaches a thick consistency but still drizzles off a knife. Spread the icing over the top and sides of the cake and leave to set before serving. This cake keeps well for 3–4 days in an airtight container.

Lynn Hill
Founder of
Clandestine Cake Club

Amid a cloud of secrecy, the Walt Disney World resort in Orlando, Florida finally opened its doors in 1971, more than 10 years after the idea for a second Disney complex had been conceived. Covering over 27,000 acres, this enchanting, fairytale paradise is said to be the most visited holiday resort in the world, with themed parks, life-sized walking talking characters, rides, water worlds, hotels and so much more. With the fresh zingy flavour of Florida's famous key limes, this 'practically perfect' chocolate cake is guaranteed to make all your cakey dreams come true.

CHOCOLATE KEY LIME CAKE

SERVES 8–10

200g unsalted butter, softened

225g caster sugar

4 medium eggs, lightly beaten

175g self-raising flour

50ml buttermilk

50g cocoa powder

1 tsp baking powder

grated zest of 2 key limes
(or regular limes)
and juice of 1

LIME CURD

170g caster sugar

60g unsalted butter, diced

grated zest and juice of 3 key limes (or regular limes)

2 medium eggs

FILLING AND TOPPING

250g mascarpone cheese

200ml double cream

1 tbsp icing sugar, plus extra to dust

grated zest of 1 lime, to decorate

1. Preheat the oven to 200°C/fan 180°C/gas 6. Grease and line two 18cm sandwich tins.

2. Start by making the curd. Place all the ingredients apart from the eggs in a heatproof bowl set over a pan of simmering water. Ensure the bottom of the bowl does not touch the water. Whisk the mixture well to combine, then add the eggs. Continue to stir as the curd gradually thickens; it will take 20–30 minutes. When the curd is thick enough to coat the back of a spoon quite thickly, strain through a sieve into a bowl. Allow to cool completely.

3. Beat the butter and sugar using a wooden spoon or electric whisk, until light and fluffy. Gradually add the eggs together with a little flour to help prevent curdling. Add the buttermilk and fold in the remaining flour, cocoa powder and baking powder. Add the lime zest and juice and mix until well combined.

4. Divide between the tins and bake for 20–25 minutes or until a skewer inserted in the centre of the cakes come out clean. Leave in the tins to cool for about 10 minutes before turning out on to a wire rack to cool completely.

5. Make the filling. Loosen the mascarpone by beating with a wooden spoon. Lightly whip the cream and add to the mascarpone along with the icing sugar, then mix until thick and smooth. If the mixture is too thick, add a little more (un-whipped) cream.

6. Spread about a third of the filling mixture on top of one cake layer, followed by a generous covering of lime curd. Place the second cake layer on top, transfer the remaining filling mixture to a piping bag and pipe over the top. When ready to serve, dust with icing sugar and scatter over grated some lime zest.

Diwali is an ancient Hindu festival honouring Lakshmi, the goddess of wealth. The word 'Diwali' means 'rows of lighted lamps' and it is a vibrant, colourful festival when Hindus decorate their houses and shops with lamps and leave their windows open to invite Lakshmi and her wealth inside. Gifts of sweets are exchanged, the milk-based 'barfi' being a traditional choice. Why not prepare your own Diwali celebration and bake this nutty cake, inspired by the confection. Chintal has used milk powder to mimic the taste of a barfi, while a white chocolate buttercream and a jewel-like pistachio and bright orange zest topping give the cake a celebratory air.

Chintal Kakaya

PISTACHIO AND COCONUT BARFI CAKE

SERVES 12

315g self-raising flour

60g milk powder

1½ tsp baking powder

200g caster sugar

1 tsp ground cardamom

25g pistachios, toasted and roughly crushed

20g desiccated coconut

250ml vegetable oil

300ml whole milk

BUTTERCREAM

100g good-quality white chocolate, roughly broken up

250g salted butter, at room temperature

400g icing sugar, sifted

1 tsp orange extract

1–2 tbsp milk

DECORATION

4 tbsp desiccated coconut, toasted

3 tbsp pistachios, toasted and roughly chopped

grated zest of 2 oranges

1. Preheat the oven to 190°C/fan 170°C/gas 5. Grease and line a deep 20cm springform cake tin.

2. In a large bowl, sift together the flour, milk powder, baking powder, sugar and cardamom, then add the pistachios and coconut. Using a balloon whisk, stir the dry mixture until the ingredients are well mixed. Pour in the oil and milk and stir into a smooth batter.

3. Pour the batter into the cake tin and bake in the middle of the oven for 40–50 minutes or until a skewer inserted in the centre of the cake comes out clean. Cool in the tin for 5 minutes before turning out on to a wire rack to cool completely.

4. To make the buttercream, place the chocolate in a heatproof bowl set over a pan of simmering water and leave to melt. Set aside to cool.

5. In a separate bowl, beat the butter with an electric whisk for 2 minutes on a medium speed, until lighter in colour and creamy. Add the icing sugar in three parts, beating well after each addition. Add the orange extract and one tablespoon of the milk between additions of the sugar. Continue beating while you add the cooled chocolate and beat until smooth. The buttercream should be spreadable, but if you want a firmer buttercream, add some more icing sugar or, if you want to loosen it, beat in the other tablespoon of milk.

6. To assemble, slice your cake in half horizontally so you have two layers. Using a palette knife, spread the buttercream over one sponge half and sandwich with the other, then cover the whole cake with the remainder. Decorate by sprinkling over the coconut, pistachios and orange zest.

Apples are an item that many of us pop into our supermarket trolley automatically, but we've probably chosen from only four or five different types. There are in fact around 1,900 varieties of English apple but tragically many of these are in danger because of the small selection made available to us commercially. Apple Day was created in 1990 to celebrate and demonstrate the diversity of apples grown in the UK. Techniques for growing the best quality of apple were honed during the eighteenth century so it seems appropriate to celebrate this important day by baking a cake inspired by an eighteenth-century 'receipt' for taffety tart, an historical recipe that Martine loves so much that she couldn't resist including a similar version in her novel, *An Appetite for Violets*. Be sure to seek out locally grown apples to help preserve our orchards and celebrate the many different varieties they can bear.

Martine Bailey

TAFFETY CAKE

SERVES 10

2 medium sweet red apples
(see above)

juice of 1 lemon

150g unsalted butter, softened

150g caster sugar

1 tsp vanilla extract

finely grated zest of 1 orange

4 medium eggs

200g plain flour

1 tsp baking powder

pinch of fine salt

60ml milk

1–2 tsp rose water, or to taste
(optional)

1 x 340g jar of quince jam
(Tiptree is excellent)

1. Preheat the oven to 180°C/fan 160°C/gas 4. Grease and line a 22cm springform cake tin.

2. Slice the apples thinly (you should have about 24 slices per apple). Toss the slices in the lemon juice to prevent browning.

3. Using an electric whisk, beat the butter, sugar, vanilla extract and orange zest until light and creamy. Add the eggs one at a time, beating well after each addition.

4. In a separate bowl, sift the flour, baking powder and salt together. Add half the flour mixture to the butter mixture and stir well. Add the milk and 1 teaspoon of the rose water, being careful to add it slowly and tasting as you go, as brands have different strengths. Add the rest of the flour mixture, and mix until the batter is smooth, though still quite liquid.

5. Place the quince jam in a small saucepan over a low heat and leave it to melt and liquefy. Pass the jam through a sieve into a bowl. Stir the unsieved chunks of quince into the batter and reserve the liquid.

6. Spoon the batter into the tin. Arrange the apple slices in overlapping circles on top of the batter. Bake for about 1 hour, or until a skewer inserted in the centre of the cake comes out clean. If it looks as though it is browning too quickly cover the top with foil. Leave in the tin for 10 minutes before turning out on to a wire rack to cool.

7. Re-melt the sieved quince glaze if necessary, adding the final teaspoon of rose water, if you wish, and brush over the surface of the cooled cake.

Hallowe'en-themed Cake Club events are very popular at this time of year. Members become evermore adventurous with their baking, creating cakes inspired by ghosts, ghouls, witches and wizards, which sit alongside elaborately carved jack-o'-lanterns on tables festooned with spiders' webs. Don't waste the pumpkin flesh from your own carved creations, use it to bake this warming spiced pumpkin cake, devised by Jen using pumpkins grown by her dad. Let others brave the cold for an evening of trick or treating, while you sit back and enjoy your own homemade treat – an irresistible slice of this autumnal delight.

Jen Dyke

SPICED PUMPKIN CAKE

SERVES 12

450g plain flour, sifted

350g soft light brown sugar

4 tsp baking powder

1 tbsp ground cinnamon

1½ tsp ground nutmeg

1 tsp ground ginger

pinch of salt

4 medium eggs

240ml vegetable oil

400g raw pumpkin, puréed (pop it in the blender or mash it)

2 tsp vanilla extract

FILLING AND DECORATION

75g butter

grated zest and juice of 1 lemon

200g icing sugar

750g ready-to-roll sugarpaste

orange, green and brown gel food colourings

1. Preheat the oven to 180°C/fan 160°C/gas 4. Thoroughly grease two 16cm hemisphere tins.

2. Mix all the dry ingredients together in a bowl. Add the eggs, oil, pumpkin and vanilla and mix until just combined (it doesn't need to be smooth).

3. Divide the mixture between the tins, leaving a 2cm gap at the top of each, and bake for 45–60 minutes or until a skewer inserted in the centre of the cakes comes out clean. Allow to cool in the tins for 15 minutes, then turn out on to a wire rack to cool completely.

4. Once cool, trim the flatter sides of the two cakes, so that they fit together neatly. Trim a small amount off the rounded end of one cake, to give a flatter bottom so that it will sit securely on a plate. From the other cake, cut a small dimple in the rounded end; this is where the stalk will sit.

5. Beat together the butter, lemon zest and juice and icing sugar, to give a smooth buttercream. Sandwich the cakes together with a very thin layer of buttercream. Using a palette knife, cover the whole cake with a very thin layer of frosting – a 'crumb coat'. Refrigerate for at least 30 minutes.

6. Set aside 50g of sugarpaste for the decorations, and colour the remainder orange. Use a piece of string to measure the circumference of the cake, and roll out the sugarpaste to a circle a little larger than this – it should be no more than 4–5mm thick.

7. Put the sugarpaste over the cake and, starting with the top, gently smooth and stretch with your hands to get an even finish. If there are any loose ends they can be tucked away under the bottom of the cake.

8. Use the handle of a paintbrush or something similar and gently press lines into the cake to mark the ribs/ridges running from top to bottom. Divide the reserved sugarpaste in half, and colour one half brown and the other green. Shape the brown section into a fat cylinder, for the stalk, then secure to the top of the cake with a little water.

9. Use a knife or cutter to make leaf shapes from the green sugarpaste, and stick them at one side of the cake, using a dab of water.

NOVEMBER

Early November
DAY OF THE DEAD
TRIPLE CHOCOLATE
CAKE OF DEATH

4th November
MARGUERITE PATTEN'S
BIRTHDAY (1915)
QUICK FRUIT CAKE

5th November
GUY FAWKES' NIGHT
STICKY CINDER TOFFEE CAKE

11th November
ARMISTICE DAY
POPPY CAKE

13th November
4TH EARL OF SANDWICH'S
BIRTHDAY (1718)
BLUEBERRY SANDWICH CAKE
WITH LEMON BUTTERCREAM

15th November
NATIONAL BUNDT DAY
PASSION FRUIT CAIPIRINHA
BUNDT CAKE

Mid to late November
CHILDREN IN NEED
POLKA DOT CAKE

Late November
THANKSGIVING
SWEET POTATO CAKE
WITH SPICED VANILLA
BUTTERCREAM

30th November
ST ANDREW'S DAY
BUTTERMILK RASPBERRY
SHORTCAKE

Gary Morton

The Día de los Muertos (Day of the Dead) originated in Mexico but is now celebrated all over South America. It is a joyful celebration when friends and family gather to remember the lives of loved ones by enjoying food, drink and parties, with symbols such as sugar skulls and chocolate skeletons offered up to the dead on altars or mantelpieces. Chocolate is native to Central America and the idea of grinding cacao beans to make hot chocolate came from the Mayans and Aztecs. Hot chocolate is still drunk in abundance in Mexico, particularly on this day in November when the colder weather is starting to set in. For a more decadent contribution to Day of the Dead festivities, why not bake this lavishly rich chocolate cake? With its dark chocolate ganache coating and scattering of chocolate shavings, this cake will certainly provide a spirited celebration as you remember your loved ones.

TRIPLE CHOCOLATE CAKE OF DEATH

SERVES 10

7 medium eggs

430g caster sugar

430g unsalted butter, softened

380g self-raising flour

50g cocoa powder

GANACHE

425ml double cream

3 tbsp golden caster sugar

300g dark chocolate (minimum 70 per cent cocoa solids), roughly broken up

DECORATION

100g white chocolate, finely shaved

100g milk chocolate, finely shaved

thin shards of white and milk chocolate (optional)

1. Start by making the ganache. Heat the cream and sugar until just below boiling point. Remove from the heat, then slowly stir in the chocolate and allow to melt until fully incorporated. Allow to cool to room temperature, then transfer to the fridge for 1–2 hours or until it thickens.

2. Preheat the oven to 180°C/fan 160°C/gas 4. Grease and line three 18cm sandwich tins.

3. Place all the sponge ingredients in a bowl and, using an electric hand whisk, beat them together until a smooth batter forms. Divide the mixture equally between the tins and bake for about 40 minutes, until a skewer inserted in the centre of the cakes comes out clean. Leave in the tins for 10–15 minutes, then turn out on to a wire rack to cool completely.

4. To decorate and assemble, decide which cake layer will be the top layer – it should be the flattest. Trim the cakes with a serrated knife if necessary. Spread a few spoonfuls of ganache over the first layer, then add the middle layer and repeat the process. Add the top layer and spread a layer of ganache over the top. Use a palette knife to cover the sides of the cake in a layer of ganache, then transfer to the fridge for 20 minutes to firm up. Repeat with another layer of ganache and chill for a further 20 minutes. This should ensure the cake has a smooth covering. Stick the white and milk chocolate shavings all over the cake and add any shards, if using.

Marguerite Patten CBE is considered one of the earliest 'celebrity chefs'. The venerable food writer and home economist presented her first cookery programme in 1947 and went on to become a bestselling cookery writer – over 17 million copies of her books have been sold around the world! Perhaps most famously, Marguerite Patten worked for the Ministry of Food during the Second World War, advising BBC radio listeners how to cook nourishing and inventive meals from their wartime rations. In homage to a queen of practicality and economy, Sue has created this quick and easy fruit cake. It packs in all the plump juicy fruits and flavours of a traditional fruit cake, without the lengthy soaking time these normally require. A quick store-cupboard fix, it is ideal for celebrating any occasion, but particularly perfect for the birthday of Britain's most famous frugal baker.

Susan Jones

QUICK FRUIT CAKE

SERVES 10

340g mixed dried fruit (such as currants, sultanas, raisins and dates)

170g margarine

170g golden granulated sugar

280ml cold water

225g self-raising flour, sifted

½ tsp ground ginger

1 tsp mixed spice

½ tsp freshly grated nutmeg

2 large eggs, beaten

1 x 250g packet ready-to-roll sugarpaste

1. Preheat the oven to 180°C/fan 160°C/gas 4. Grease and line a 900g loaf tin.

2. Place the fruit, margarine, sugar and water in a saucepan. Bring to the boil and simmer for 10 minutes. This will plump up the fruit. Strain the fruit, reserving the liquid, then transfer the fruit to a large mixing bowl and leave until cool.

3. Add the flour and spices to the fruit and mix well, then add the beaten egg. Add enough of the reserved fruit cooking liquid to give the mixture a dropping consistency. Pour into the tin and bake for 1¼ hours or until a skewer inserted in the centre of the cake comes out clean. Leave to cool in the tin for a few minutes, then turn out on to a wire rack to cool completely.

4. When the cake has completely cooled, roll out the sugarpaste to your desired thickness, then cut out shapes for quick and easy decoration or cover the whole cake for a more classic finish.

Guy Fawkes is the most famous conspirator in the notorious 'gunpowder plot'. On the 5th November 1605 he and his fellow accomplices attempted to blow up the Houses of Parliament and assassinate James I and his family. When the plot was uncovered, Fawkes was sentenced to a traitor's death – to be 'hanged, drawn and quartered' – and bonfires were burned around the country in celebration of the king's lucky escape. The date became an occasion of thanksgiving and celebration, and nowadays effigies of Guy Fawkes are burned on bonfires around the UK accompanied by extravagant firework displays. Ensure your Guy Fawkes' Night goes with a bang by baking this spectacular sticky toffee cake. Be careful when making the cinder toffee – adding the bicarbonate of soda to hot caramel can create quite an explosion of bubbles!

Alison Holden-Jones

STICKY CINDER TOFFEE CAKE

SERVES 10–12

400g dried prunes

150ml hot water

350g self-raising flour

1 tsp bicarbonate of soda

160g unsalted butter

200g soft light brown sugar or light muscovado sugar

100g soft dark brown sugar or dark muscovado sugar

4 large eggs, lightly beaten

2 tsp vanilla extract

CINDER TOFFEE

vegetable oil, for the tin

150g caster sugar

75g golden syrup

1½ tsp bicarbonate of soda

> *Ingredients and recipe continue overleaf*

1. Start by making the cinder toffee. Grease and line a shallow baking tray. Gently heat the sugar and golden syrup in a large heavy-based pan until all the sugar has dissolved. Turn up the heat and rapidly boil – do not stir the mixture, just swirl the pan if it starts to go darker on one side. Keep boiling until the mixture turns a lovely golden brown colour – it should take approximately 5 minutes. Remove from the heat. Add the bicarbonate of soda and stir for a few seconds, being very careful as the mixture will bubble, fizz and expand quite a bit. Tip the mixture into the baking tray and leave to set.

2. Preheat the oven to 180°C/fan 160°C/gas 4. Grease and line two 23cm cake tins.

3. Put the prunes in a bowl and cover with the hot water. Leave to soak for 20 minutes or so, then blend until very smooth.

4. Sift the flour and bicarbonate of soda into a bowl. In a separate bowl, beat the butter and sugars until pale and fluffy. Add the egg a little at a time, adding a spoonful of flour between additions to prevent any curdling. Fold in the remaining flour, add the prune mixture and vanilla extract and stir thoroughly. Pour into the tins and bake for 35–40 minutes or until a skewer inserted in the centre of the cakes comes out clean. Remove from the oven and leave to cool in the tins. >

CARAMEL SAUCE

55g unsalted butter, chopped
into pieces

175g light muscovado sugar

225ml double cream

1 tbsp golden syrup

BUTTERCREAM

320g unsalted butter, softened

400g icing sugar, sifted

2 tsp vanilla extract

5. To make the caramel sauce, place the butter, sugar and half the cream in a saucepan and melt over a medium heat. Once melted, turn up the heat slightly and bring to the boil, stirring constantly, until the sugar dissolves. Add the golden syrup and let the sauce bubble away for a couple of minutes.

6. Remove from the heat and leave to cool a little before stirring in the remaining cream.

7. For the buttercream, beat the butter, icing sugar and vanilla extract for around 5 minutes with an electric whisk and add 4 tablespoons of the cooled caramel sauce.

8. To assemble, put the cinder toffee in a bag and bash it to break it up ready for decorating. Remove the cooled cakes from the tins. Spread 4 heaped tablespoons of buttercream over the base layer and place the second layer on top. Spread a thin layer of the buttercream over the whole cake (leave enough buttercream for piping round the edge of the top of the cake), then press the cinder toffee crumbs around the sides. Transfer the remaining buttercream to a disposable piping bag fitted with a rosette nozzle and pipe small stars all the way round the edge of the top of the cake. Fill the top of the cake with larger smashed-up pieces of cinder toffee and drizzle caramel sauce over the buttercream stars.

Note

This makes more caramel sauce than is needed for the cake but you can always find a use for amazing caramel sauce – pour over ice cream, dip fresh fruit in it or just eat straight from the jug!

Children in Need is the BBC's corporate charity, famously represented by its bright yellow mascot, Pudsey Bear, who wears a spotted eye bandage. The charity provides grants to organisations supporting disadvantaged children and young people around the UK. Every November, celebrities gear up for Children in Need night, an evening of televised entertainment that helps raise money for the telethon appeal. Bake sales are a popular way to fundraise and many get underway well before the night itself. This recipe is an easy and fun way to get involved. Have fun covering the bright yellow sponge cake with colourful polka dots to match Pudsey's patch and watch as children delight in the crunchy surprise in the centre of the cake.

Lynn Hill
Founder of
Clandestine Cake Club

POLKA DOT CAKE

SERVES 8–10

225g unsalted butter, softened

225g caster sugar

4 medium eggs

225g self-raising flour

1 tsp vanilla extract

2 tbsp milk (optional)

yellow gel food colouring

FILLING AND TOPPING

50g double cream

1 x 165g packet M&M's chocolate

5 tbsp lemon curd

2 tbsp apricot jam

1 x 450g packet ready-rolled white sugarpaste

3 x small blocks (100g) ready-to-roll sugarpaste in different colours

icing sugar, to dust

1. Preheat the oven to 190°C/fan 170°C/gas 5. Grease and line two 20cm loose-bottomed sandwich tins

2. Beat the butter and sugar using a wooden spoon or electric whisk until light and fluffy. Add the eggs one at a time, beating well after each addition, and adding a tablespoon of flour with the final egg to prevent curdling. Fold in the remaining flour. Add the vanilla extract and mix until well combined. You should have a dropping consistency; if not, gradually add the milk until this is achieved. Slowlyly add drops of the food colouring and mix until the batter is a bright yellow. Divide the mixture between the two sandwich tins and bake for 20–25 minutes or until a skewer inserted in the centre of the cake comes out clean. Leave to cool in the tins for 10 minutes before turning out on to a wire rack to cool completely.

3. Gently whip the cream and spread this over the top of one of the cake layers, then scatter the M&M's over the cream. Spread the curd over the top of the second cake, invert and sandwich the two layers together so that the smooth base layer is uppermost. This will give you a good flat surface for the sugarpaste. Place the jam in a pan and heat gently. Take off the heat and sieve the jam, then leave to cool a little.

4. Place the cake on a board and brush the top and sides of the cake with the cooled jam – this will help the sugarpaste stick to the cake. Cover the cake with the white sugarpaste, smoothing down the top and sides and over any visible parts of the cake board.

5. Knead the coloured sugarpastes until soft enough to roll, then roll out as before. Cut out different sized coloured circles. Using cooled boiled water, stick the circles all over the cake. Cut out a thin ribbon of coloured sugarpaste and wrap around the base of the cake to finish the decoration.

Suzanne Woodruff

Armistice Day marks the end of hostilities on the Western Front and the armistice signed by the Allies and Germany on 11th November 1918, which signalled the end of the First World War. The scarlet poppy is emblematic of the blood spilled during the war since the flower was the only one to bloom across the battlefields of Flanders. Decorated with its own wreath of sugarpaste poppies, this light poppy seed cake is a simple token to accompany your own celebration of remembrance.

POPPY CAKE

SERVES 8

175g caster sugar

3 large eggs

175g solid vegetable fat
(such as Stork) or butter, softened

175g self-raising flour

1 tsp baking powder

2 tbsp poppy seeds

FILLING

4 tbsp raspberry jam

75g solid vegetable fat
(such as Stork) or butter, softened

150g icing sugar, sifted

1 tsp vanilla extract

1 tbsp milk

DECORATION

2 tbsp apricot jam

450g ready-to-roll white
sugarpaste

ready-to roll sugarpaste
in red, green and black

icing sugar, to dust

1. Preheat the oven to 160°C/fan 140°C/gas 3. Grease and line a 20cm cake tin.

2. Using an electric whisk, beat the sugar and eggs until creamy. Add the remaining sponge ingredients and beat until thoroughly combined and smooth. Spoon into the prepared tin and tap the tin on the work surface to level the top. Place on the middle oven shelf and bake for 50–60 minutes, until a skewer inserted in the centre of the cake comes out clean. Cool in the tin for 10–15 minutes, then turn out on to a wire rack to cool completely.

3. Once cool, slice the cake into two layers. Place the base of the cake on a plate or board. Spread the raspberry jam over the base right up to the edges.

4. Place the vegetable fat in a bowl and soften slightly with the back of a wooden spoon. Gradually add the icing sugar and beat well until a smooth buttercream forms. Stir in the vanilla extract. Add the milk and beat in to loosen the buttercream a little.

5. Spread the buttercream over the cut side of the top half of the cake and place on top of the jam, pressing together lightly. Set the cake aside, while you prepare the decoration.

6. Warm the apricot jam in a small pan over a low heat. Knead the white sugarpaste until soft enough to roll out. Place on a work surface, lightly dusted with icing sugar, and roll into roughly a 20cm circle, 3–4mm thick. Using the cake tin as a template, cut out a circle to fit the top of the cake.

7. Spread the top of the cake lightly with some apricot jam. Add the circle of icing and press down to cover the top of the cake.

8. Knead the green block of icing to soften, then roll out until thin. Use a sharp knife to cut out 8 leaf shapes. Spread some of the apricot jam over the back of each leaf and stick them around the top of the cake.

9. Knead and roll out the red icing as before. Either use a flower cutter to stamp out four flower shapes or cut out circles and make your own poppies as in the photo opposite. Stick the poppies on to the cake with apricot jam.

10. Roll four small balls of the black icing and, using a dab of apricot jam, stick each one into the centre of each poppy flower to complete the decoration. The cake will keep for 3–4 days in an airtight container.

A Bundt refers to any type of cake baked in a Bundt tin. The iconic ring shape was inspired by northern European fruit breads known as *Gugelhupf*, which were made in ceramic ring moulds. During the 1950s and 60s, American cookware brand NordicWare started producing similar-shaped tins made from cast aluminium and trademarked the name 'Bundt'. The striking design has become so popular that there is now a national Bundt Day, when fans of these ornate tins fire up their ovens for an extravagance of baking. Club member Rachel McGrath is a passionate Bundt tin collector and avid baker of all things Bundt. Her cocktail-flavoured creation, with its bright glaze, designed to show off every detail of its elegant shape, is the ideal cake to celebrate the occasion. To bake successfully in Bundt tins: grease them with a cake release spray, making sure you get into all the elements of the design; never fill your tin more than three-quarters full; and leave your cake to cool in the tin for at least 10 minutes before turning out on to a wire rack to cool completely.

Rachel McGrath

PASSION FRUIT CAIPIRINHA BUNDT CAKE

SERVES 12–16

cake release spray, for the tin

225g unsalted butter

450g golden caster sugar

4 medium eggs

1 tsp lemon extract

couple of drops of orange blossom extract

grated zest of 1 lime

3 tbsp ready-made passion fruit caipirinha cocktail mix, plus 125ml extra for the topping

350g plain flour

½ tsp bicarbonate of soda

½ tsp salt

250ml passion fruit yoghurt (try to get one with a layer of coulis)

300g icing sugar

yellow gel food colouring

1. Preheat the oven to 160°C/fan 140°C/gas 3. Spray a 25 x 7cm Bundt tin with cake release spray and dust with flour.

2. Beat the butter and sugar using an electric whisk, until light and fluffy. Add the eggs one at a time, beating well after each addition. Add the lemon and orange extracts, lime zest and caipirinha mix.

3. In a separate bowl, sift together the flour, bicarbonate of soda and salt. Pour the yoghurt into a jug.

4. Fold a third of the flour mixture into the creamed mix, followed by half the yoghurt. Repeat until everything is combined. Give everything a quick mix with an electric whisk on a low speed for about 10 seconds, then pour the mix into your prepared tin.

5. Bake in the centre of the oven for 1¼ hours or until a skewer inserted in the centre of the cake comes out clean. Leave the cake to cool in the tin for 10 minutes before turning out on to a wire rack to cool completely.

6. To finish, mix the icing sugar with enough of the ready-made caipirinha mix to make a runny glaze, and add a little yellow food colouring. Use a spoon to drizzle the glaze over the cake.

Notes

You can buy ready-made caipirinha in 250ml pouches from the supermarket; one brand is Parrot Bay. This can be made in any shaped Bundt tin of a similar size.

John Montague, the 4th Earl of Sandwich, is credited with the invention of one of our favourite lunchtime foods. So engrossed was the Earl in his game of cards one evening, that he didn't want to break for dinner. He instructed his cook to bring him some sustenance between two slices of bread so that he could keep his hands – and his cards – clean while he carried on with his game. Not content with savoury sandwiches, some sweet-toothed spark decided to make their 'sandwich' out of cake, and so a classic was born. Make a change from the Victoria sandwich (see page 149) and enjoy this fruity little twist. But don't expect your fingers to stay clean – bursts of blueberries and a creamy lemon filling make it impossible to keep your hands off this one.

Gemma Underwood

BLUEBERRY SANDWICH CAKE WITH LEMON BUTTERCREAM

SERVES 8–10

225g unsalted butter

225g caster sugar

225g self-raising flour, sifted, plus a little extra to dust

3 medium eggs, whisked

1 tsp vanilla essence

225g fresh blueberries

LEMON BUTTERCREAM

110g unsalted butter, softened

350g icing sugar, plus extra to dust

3 tbsp lemon juice

1. Preheat the oven to 200°C/fan 180°C/gas 6. Grease and line two square 18cm baking tins.

2. Beat the butter and sugar using a wooden spoon or electric whisk, until light and fluffy. Add the flour and whisked egg alternately a little at a time, until thoroughly combined. Add the vanilla and mix well.

3. Wash the blueberries and lightly coat them in the extra flour, then gently fold them into the mixture.

4. Divide the mixture between the tins. Bake for 25–30 minutes or until a skewer inserted in the centre of the cakes comes out clean. Leave in their tins to cool.

5. For the buttercream, beat the butter and half the icing sugar, then add the lemon juice and mix again. Add the rest of the icing sugar and beat well, until smooth. Remove the cakes from the tins and spread the buttercream over one of the cakes. Gently place the other cake on top and dust with icing sugar to serve.

Many people trace the date of the USA's first Thanksgiving to the autumn of 1621, when the Pilgrims celebrated a bountiful harvest and feasted for three days. However, it wasn't until the late 1600s that giving thanks for a harvest became established as an annual event. Today Thanksgiving is celebrated on the fourth Thursday in November and is one of America's biggest national holidays – an abundant, extravagant celebration culminating in a huge feast as families gather to give thanks for what they have. The centrepiece of a traditional Thanksgiving meal is a turkey, which is what the Pilgrims were thought to have enjoyed, while other staples on the table include side dishes and desserts made from sweet potato, a food native to North America. This spiced sweet potato cake is delicately fragrant; it would be an interesting twist on the more traditional pumpkin pie finish to a Thanksgiving celebration.

Jen Storey

SWEET POTATO CAKE
WITH SPICED VANILLA BUTTERCREAM

SERVES 12

375g plain flour

2 scant tsp baking powder

½ tsp bicarbonate of soda

½ tsp salt

½ tsp ground cinnamon

¼ tsp ground nutmeg

¼ tsp ground ginger

225g unsalted butter, at room temperature

400g caster sugar

400g cooled, peeled baked sweet potatoes, passed through a sieve (see Note)

1 tsp vanilla extract

2 tsp vegetable oil

4 large eggs, at room temperature

1. Preheat the oven to 170°C/fan 150°C/gas 3. Grease and flour two 23cm cake tins.

2. Sift together the flour, baking powder, bicarbonate of soda, salt, cinnamon, nutmeg and ginger. Set aside.

3. In large mixing bowl, beat the butter and sugar using an electric whisk, until light and fluffy. Add the sweet potato purée and vanilla and beat until well blended. Add the oil, then add the eggs, one at a time (the batter will look curdled). Add the flour mixture very slowly, beating on a low speed until just combined. Do not overmix.

4. Pour the batter into the tins. Bake in the oven for 30–35 minutes or until a skewer inserted into the centre of the cakes comes out clean. Cool in the tins for 10 minutes, then turn out on to wire racks to cool completely.

BUTTERCREAM

170g unsalted butter, at room temperature

225g cream cheese, at room temperature

1 vanilla pod, seeds scraped

½ tsp ground cinnamon

480g icing sugar

5. For the buttercream, mix the butter and cream cheese using an electric whisk set at a medium speed, until fluffy. Add the vanilla seeds and ground cinnamon and continue to mix on a low speed until smooth. Gradually add the icing sugar until you reach a spreadable buttercream consistency.

6. To assemble, first level your cakes. It can help to chill your cakes for this as it makes them easier to handle. Using a serrated knife, cut off any dome or excess from the top of your cake. Place one cake on a cake plate and use a palette knife to cover it with a layer of buttercream. Add the second cake layer, then cover the whole cake with a very thin layer of buttercream – a 'crumb coat'. Set aside for 20–30 minutes, then cover with a full layer of buttercream.

Note

It is important to pass the sweet potato through a fine mesh sieve before you measure it out. Sweet potatoes are naturally pulpy and would make a very unsatisfactory texture for a cake if you didn't strain them. You can even use a baby's sweet potato purée, which works the best.

Lynn Hill
Founder of
Clandestine Cake Club

The Scottish are renowned for their love of a good knees-up, so the day of their patron saint, Andrew, is marked with hearty good cheer. It's an official bank holiday and is celebrated with pageantry, dining and Celtic dancing, as Scots 'strip the willow' and seek out their 'dashing white sergeant' at traditional ceilidhs. Crisp, buttery shortbread is a Scotch national treasure, while some of Britain's best and most flavoursome raspberries are grown in the country's cool climate. It seems fitting to celebrate St Andrew's Day in bounteous style by baking this cake made from the best of Scotland's larder. (Pictured overleaf.)

BUTTERMILK RASPBERRY SHORTCAKE

SERVES 8–12

125g unsalted butter, softened

125g caster sugar

1 medium egg, lightly beaten

120g self-raising flour

30g ground almonds

100ml buttermilk

CRÈME PATISSIÈRE

60g caster sugar

2 medium egg yolks

30g cornflour

200ml semi-skimmed or full-fat milk, plus 2 tbsp

1 vanilla pod, seeds scraped

60g unsalted butter

1. Start by making the crème patissière. In a large bowl, whisk together the sugar and egg yolks until lighter in colour and creamy. Mix the cornflour with the 2 tablespoons of cold milk until combined. Add to the egg mixture and give it a good mix.

2. Pour the 200ml of milk into a pan and add the vanilla pod and seeds. Heat gently over a low heat until bubbles appear at the side of the pan. Take off the heat and pour the milk through a sieve into the egg mixture, whisking all the time.

3. Pour the mixture back into the pan and cook gently over a low heat, whisking constantly to avoid lumps. The mixture will soon begin to thicken. Once thick enough to coat the back of a spoon, take off the heat, add the butter and give it a good whisk until nice and smooth and all the butter has melted. Pour into a bowl, cover the surface with cling film to avoid a skin forming and cool in the fridge.

4. Make the shortbread. Preheat the oven to 200°C/fan 180°C/gas 6. Draw a 20cm square on a piece of baking parchment, turn it over and place the paper on a greased baking tray.

5. Put the flour, butter and sugar in a bowl and beat until the consistency is like breadcrumbs. Beat a little more until everything comes together into a ball. Press the mixture on to the baking parchment within the marked square and bake for 12–15 minutes or until pale in colour and firm to the touch. (Leave the oven at this temperature.)

6. Leave on the tray for 3–4 minutes, then square off the four edges and cut the shortbread into 32 even triangles. Do this by cutting out a square grid of 4 x 4 squares, then cutting lines diagonally across the square until you have

SHORTBREAD

175g plain flour

125g unsalted butter, softened

60g golden caster sugar, plus a
little extra to dust

TOPPING

250g raspberries

icing sugar, to dust

enough triangle shapes. Dust with caster sugar and leave on the tray to cool completely. It is essential that you slice the shortbread while still warm. If left until cold, the shortbread would crumble. For sharper edges you could score the triangles on to the shortbread before you put it in the oven.

7. Grease and line the base of a 20cm square loose-bottomed cake tin.

8. Beat the butter and sugar together with a wooden spoon or electric whisk, until light and creamy. Gradually add the egg, beating well and adding a tablespoon of the flour to help prevent curdling. Fold in the remaining flour, the ground almonds and buttermilk. Gently mix until well combined.

9. Pour the mix into the tin and bake for 20 minutes or until a skewer inserted in the centre of the cake comes out clean. Leave in the tin for 10 minutes to cool a little before carefully turning out on to a wire rack to cool completely (it's quite a fragile cake so handle it carefully).

10. To assemble, put the crème patissière into a piping bag fitted with your favourite nozzle and pipe even lines over the top of the cake, alternating with lines of the shortbread biscuits, pointing up. Dot the raspberries over the crème patissière and dust with icing sugar.

DECEMBER

1st–24th December
ADVENT

SPICED CHOCOLATE
ORANGE YULE LOG

11th December
FIRST CLANDESTINE
CAKE CLUB EVENT (2010)

CORNUCOPIA CAKE

13th December
FEAST OF ST LUCIA

NORDIC SPICE CAKE

16th December
JANE AUSTEN'S
BIRTHDAY (1775)

APRICOT AND
RATAFIA CAKE

16th December
BOSTON TEA PARTY
(1773)

BOSTON CREAM PIE

16th–24th December
LAS POSADAS

PIÑATA CAKE

20th December
PUBLICATION OF GRIMM'S
FAIRY TALES (1812)

GINGERBREAD VILLAGE
CAKE

21st December
WINTER SOLSTICE

WINTER SOLSTICE
CAKE

24th December
CHRISTMAS EVE

VANILLA SNOWFLAKE
CAKE

25th December
CHRISTMAS DAY

WALNUT AND
CRANBERRY STOLLEN

26th December
BOXING DAY

FROZEN BOX
OF DELICIOUSNESS

31st December
HOGMANAY

DUNDEE CAKE

The Clandestine Cake Club was founded in Leeds in December 2010. Eleven curious cake lovers attended our first event, for which the theme was 'cornucopia', baking and eating their way through an abundant array of different cakes and flavours. In homage to that first event, here is a bountiful celebratory cake piled with a medley of fruits and flavours that can be adapted for any time of year using seasonal produce and your favourite complementary liqueur. Break open the bubbly and enjoy a glass of cheer as you celebrate what thousands of members and their friends now consider a rather wonderful excuse for copious amounts of cake. Cheers!

Lynn Hill
Founder of
Clandestine Cake Club

CORNUCOPIA CAKE

SERVES 8–10

225g unsalted butter, softened

225g caster sugar

4 medium eggs, lightly beaten

225g self-raising flour

1 tbsp milk

SYRUP

3 tbsp caster sugar

4 tbsp Chambord liqueur

FROSTING

250g full-fat cream cheese

40g icing sugar, sifted

300ml double cream

4 tbsp Chambord liqueur

TOPPING AND DECORATION

4 x 70g packets of white chocolate Mikado sticks, uncoated ends sliced off

125g blueberries

seeds of 1 pomegranate

7 physalis

3 satsumas, peeled, separated into segments, all pith removed

1. Preheat the oven to 190°C/fan 170°C/gas 5. Grease and line two 20cm loose-bottomed sandwich tins.

2. Beat the butter and sugar using a wooden spoon or electric whisk, until light and fluffy. Add the eggs one at a time, beating well after each addition, and adding a tablespoon of flour with the final egg to prevent curdling. Fold in the flour, then add the milk and mix until well combined. Divide the mixture between the two tins and bake for 20–25 minutes or until a skewer inserted in the centre of the cakes comes out clean. Leave in the tins to cool for 5–10 minutes before turning out on to a wire rack to cool completely.

3. While the cakes are cooling, make the syrup. Heat the sugar and liqueur in a pan until all the sugar has melted, simmer for a few moments, then take off the heat and leave to cool a little. Drizzle two thirds of the syrup over the sponges and leave the cakes to cool completely. Set the remaining syrup aside for later.

4. Make the frosting by mixing the cream cheese and icing sugar together until just combined. In a separate bowl, whip the cream until soft peaks form. Gradually add the whipped cream to the cream cheese mixture and mix until well combined. Add the liqueur and mix until well combined.

5. To assemble, spread a third of the frosting over one layer of cake. Scatter over some pomegranate seeds and top with the second cake. Cover the whole cake with a very thin layer of frosting – a 'crumb coat'. Set aside for 20–30 minutes, then cover with a full layer, smoothing the top and sides.

6. Decorate the sides of the cake by sticking the Mikado sticks vertically all the way round the cake.

7. Toss the blueberries and pomegranate seeds in the remaining syrup, then carefully arrange on top of the cake. Sit the physalis and satsuma segments among the berries.

Victoria Johnsen

Advent, meaning 'coming' or 'arrival', is the time to prepare for Christmas. From 1st December to Christmas Eve, decorations are hung, gifts are shopped for, freezers are stocked and children open the windows of their Advent calendars, eagerly awaiting the arrival of the big day itself. Folklore tells us how a Yule log would often be burned on Christmas Eve and for the 12 days following it, to ensure good luck in the year ahead. These days Health and Safety would no doubt frown on that tradition so what better solution than a chocolate log instead? Sure to be a big hit with children, a slice of this zingy chocolate orange roll should distract them from the frenzy of anticipation – for a minute or two at least!

SPICED CHOCOLATE ORANGE YULE LOG

SERVES 8–10

200ml double cream

100g dark chocolate (minimum 55 per cent cocoa solids), snapped into pieces

100g milk chocolate, snapped into pieces

60g self-raising flour

40g cocoa powder

4 large eggs

100g caster sugar

icing sugar, to dust

1. Put the double cream in a saucepan and heat gently (do not boil). When it reaches roughly body temperature, take off the heat and drop in both chocolates. Stir until completely melted and combined, then scrape into a bowl and put aside to cool. Once at room temperature, chill in the fridge for 1–2 hours to thicken.

2. Preheat the oven to 200°C/fan 180°C/gas 6. Grease and line a 33 x 23cm Swiss roll tin, making sure the baking parchment is folded neatly at each corner for straight edges.

3. Sift the flour and cocoa into a bowl. Use an electric whisk to beat the eggs and caster sugar in another bowl. until pale, frothy and increased in volume. Carefully fold the dry mixture into the wet, being as gentle as you can to avoid knocking out the air bubbles that you have just worked hard to create.

4. Pour the cake batter evenly into the tin and level the top, then bake for 8–10 minutes in the centre of the oven. Keep an eye on the cake but don't open the door too early – when ready, it will have risen and started to come away from the sides of the tin. You can test it with a skewer, which should come out clean when inserted in the centre, or by gently touching the sponge: if it bounces back, the cake is done.

5. While the cake is baking, cut a piece of baking parchment just larger than the tin and sift icing sugar all over it. You need to roll the sponge while it is still warm, so once you have taken it out of the oven, flip it out on to the paper and peel off the lining.

ORANGE BUTTERCREAM

75g unsalted butter, softened

200g icing sugar

25g cocoa powder

2 tbsp milk

¾ tsp orange extract

1 tsp vanilla extract

½ tsp mixed spice

¼ tsp ground cinnamon

pinch of freshly grated nutmeg

6. Score the cake along the long edge nearest to you, around 2.5cm from the edge. Fold this edge in tightly and then roll the cake as tightly as you can, with the sugary paper rolled up inside. Leave to cool with the edge tucked underneath.

7. For the buttercream, start by beating the butter until creamy, then add the remaining ingredients. Mix until all the ingredients are blended and the icing has a lightly whipped but firm texture.

8. Once the cake has cooled completely and the chocolate in the fridge is firm, you can assemble. Unroll the sponge, discarding the paper, then spread the buttercream over the inside and roll back up tightly. At an angle, slice off a piece of the cake, and position this wherever you like to make your log look authentic – it's best to do this on the plate you will use for serving.

9. Using a small palette knife, spread the firmed-up chocolate mixture over the cake, covering the ends as well. Use a fork to create texture, and then dust lightly with icing sugar, or add festive decorations. The cake is best eaten fresh, as the sponge is very delicate.

St Lucia's Day, festival of lights, is a strongly Swedish celebration but is now celebrated across Scandinavia. The name 'Lucia' comes from the Latin for 'light', and according to legend, in the midst of one particularly harsh winter St Lucia brought the starving people of Sweden bread and light. She has become a symbol of hope amid darkness. The day's festivities begin in the early hours. Dressed in white and wearing a wreath of candles on her head, the eldest daughter of each household leads a procession of her siblings into the main room, bringing light to her family. Spiced cakes and biscuits are shared, served with steaming hot coffee. To mark this wonderful celebration of hope, here is an aromatic cake filled with warming Christmassy spices. Crown it with candles to brighten the dark winter days and anticipate the joy of Advent as you cut the first slice.

Lynn Hill
Founder of
Clandestine Cake Club

NORDIC SPICE CAKE

SERVES 12–14

cake release spray, for the tin

340g unsalted butter, at room temperature

100g light muscovado sugar

240g dark muscovado sugar

6 medium eggs

2 tbsp natural yoghurt

grated zest of 1 large orange

340g self-raising flour, sifted

¼ tsp ground cloves

½ tsp ground cinnamon

35ml mulled wine

icing sugar, to dust

1. Preheat the oven to 200°C/fan 180°C/gas 6. Spray a 25 x 7cm Bundt tin with cake release spray.

2. Beat the butter and sugars together with an electric whisk until light and fluffy, scraping down the sides of the bowl at intervals.

3. Lightly beat the eggs, yoghurt and orange zest together until combined. Add a tablespoon of flour to the butter and sugar mixture, then gradually add the egg and yoghurt mixture until light and fluffy, adding another tablespoon of flour if it looks as if it is curdling.

4. With the whisk on a low speed, gradually add the remaining flour and spices until well combined. Do not overbeat or you will overstretch the gluten in the flour, which may result in a dense cake.

5. Finally add the mulled wine and mix gently until combined. The mixture should be of a dropping consistency.

6. Pour the cake batter into the tin making sure it goes into all the grooves, and level out the top. Bake in the middle of the oven for 45–55 minutes or until a skewer inserted in various parts of the cake comes out clean each time.

7. When baked, remove from the oven and leave in the tin for 15–20 minutes, then turn out on to your favourite cake plate. Dust with icing sugar.

The great British cuppa is something we take for granted these days, but wind back the clock to the eighteenth century and our beloved beverage was the source of a major international dispute. In protest at the British government's high tax on tea, a group of American colonists ransacked British ships moored in Boston harbour and threw 340 chests of tea overboard – that's the equivalent of over 18 million cups of our favourite refreshment! The Boston Tea Party, as it became known, is an iconic event in British and American history and went on to inspire other similar demonstrations. Happily, a tea party today is something quite different and no modern occasion would be complete without cake. Don't be deceived by its name, this traditional Boston Cream Pie is most certainly a cake, with two simple sponges sandwiched around a creamy vanilla filling and topped with gooey chocolate ganache – it's the ideal companion to a steaming pot of tea and the perfect way to give thanks for our brew. (Pictured overleaf.)

Marie-Anne Crawley

BOSTON CREAM PIE

SERVES 8–10

250g unsalted butter, softened

250g caster sugar

4 large eggs

250g self-raising flour

1 tsp vanilla extract

2 tbsp milk

CHOCOLATE GANACHE

150g good-quality dark chocolate (minimum 70 per cent cocoa solids), roughly broken

150ml double cream

1. Start by making the ganache. Place the chocolate and cream in a bowl set over a pan of barely simmering water. Do not let the bottom of the bowl touch the water. Stir until the chocolate has melted and the mixture is smooth. Allow to cool to room temperature, then transfer to the fridge for 1–2 hours or until it thickens. Any leftover ganache can be kept in the fridge and used to top cupcakes or sandwich other cakes.

2. Next, make the crème patissière. Gently heat the milk and cream in a small saucepan along with the vanilla pod and seeds or the extract. Bring to boiling point, then immediately remove from the heat, cover with a lid and allow to stand and infuse for 15 minutes.

3. In a bowl, whisk the egg yolks and sugar until creamy, then whisk in the flour. Lift the vanilla pod out of the milk, then pour the milk into the egg mixture and whisk until smooth. Return to the saucepan and stir continuously over a low heat until the custard thickens enough to coat the back of a spoon.

4. Transfer the crème patissière to a bowl and cover the surface with cling film to avoid a skin forming. Allow to cool to room temperature before using.

CRÈME PATISSIÈRE

125ml milk

125ml double cream

1 vanilla pod, seeds scraped
or 1 tsp good-quality vanilla
extract

3 large egg yolks

50g caster sugar

1 tbsp plain flour

DECORATION

1 x 450g packet ready-rolled
white sugarpaste

5. Preheat the oven to 180°C/fan 160°C/gas 4. Grease and line two 20cm sandwich tins.

6. Beat the butter and sugar using a wooden spoon or electric whisk, until light and fluffy. Add the eggs one at a time, beating well after each addition, and adding a tablespoon of flour after each addition to prevent curdling.

7. Beat in the vanilla extract, then gradually add the remaining flour. Slowly add the milk until the mixture is loose and creamy. Divide between the tins evenly and level with a spoon or spatula. Bake for 30–35 minutes until well risen and golden brown and a skewer inserted in the centre of the cake comes out clean. Leave to cool in the tins for 5–10 minutes before turning out on to a wire rack to cool completely.

8. To assemble, sandwich the two cakes with the crème patissière, then spread the ganache over the top of the cake. Cut white stars from the sugarpaste and stick them all over the top for a star-spangled treat.

Jane Austen is arguably one of the most widely read novelists in English literature. Her eighteenth-century works of romantic fiction have become treasured volumes in homes around the globe and her famously headstrong, handsome, proud and pompous characters are household names. Austen's novels are seen as a social commentary on the Regency era, in particular on the lifestyle and lavish entertainment enjoyed by the landed gentry. Ratafia biscuits – delicate little almond bites made from egg whites – were very popular at the time, often served alongside dessert. So, in honour of the birthday of one of England's finest writers, here's an irresistible cake inspired by the delicious Georgian delicacy. A veritable ode to almonds, it conjures up images of elegant drawing rooms and is the perfect prelude to taking a turn on the lawn.

Lynn Hill
Founder of
Clandestine Cake Club

APRICOT AND RATAFIA CAKE

SERVES 10–12

4 fresh apricots, stoned
and quartered

175g soft light brown sugar,
plus 2 tbsp

3 tbsp apricot liqueur

175g self-raising flour

¼ tsp baking powder

175g unsalted butter, softened

⅛ tsp almond extract

3 medium eggs, lightly beaten

75g ratafia or amaretti biscuits

20g flaked almonds

1. Preheat the oven to 180°C/fan 160°C/gas 4. Grease and line a 20cm cake tin.

2. Place the apricots, the 2 tablespoons of brown sugar, the liqueur and 3 tablespoons of water into a pan and heat gently until the sugar has dissolved, then simmer for 5 minutes. Take off the heat and leave to one side to cool completely.

3. Sift the flour and baking powder together and leave to one side. Beat the butter and sugar using a wooden spoon or electric whisk, until light and fluffy. Add the almond extract to the beaten eggs and gradually add to the butter and sugar mixture with a little of the flour to help prevent curdling. Crush two thirds of the ratafia biscuits and mix into the batter until well combined.

4. Strain the apricots, reserving the syrup. Chop half the apricots into 5mm pieces and add to the mixture; mix until well combined. Pour the batter into the cake tin, then scatter over the remaining apricot quarters, the flaked almonds and some of the remaining whole ratafia biscuits. Crush the remaining biscuits and scatter these over too. Bake for 30 minutes, then remove, cover the tin with foil and bake for a further 20 minutes, until golden brown and a skewer inserted in the centre of the cake comes out clean.

5. Re-heat the syrup and carefully pour over the still-warm cake. Leave in the tin to cool for about 15 minutes before turning out on to a wire rack to cool completely.

For those in the northern hemisphere, the winter solstice marks the shortest day and the longest night of the year. In Britain, this means that the sun will set between 4 and 5 o'clock in the afternoon, which is of course teatime! So why not celebrate the coming of longer days and shorter nights and enjoy your afternoon cuppa with a slice of this eye-catching cake. Its midnight blue sponge, snowy white icing and jewelled sugar icicles will have you dreaming of a perfectly wintery wonderland as you enjoy a generous slice beside a nice cosy fire.

Katherine Howe

WINTER SOLSTICE CAKE

SERVES 10–12

300g self-raising flour

1 tsp baking powder

175g caster sugar

150ml sunflower oil

150ml cold water

1½ tsp vanilla extract

blue and purple gel food colouring

FROSTING AND DECORATION

20 Fox's glacier mints

blue edible glitter

150g cream cheese

450g icing sugar

1. Preheat the oven to 180°C/fan 160°C/gas 4. Grease and line two 20cm sandwich tins.

2. Sift the flour and baking powder into a bowl and stir in the sugar. Add the oil, water and vanilla and mix well.

3. Add ½ teaspoon of blue gel colouring and ¼ teaspoon of purple colouring to the batter and mix until evenly distributed. Combining these two colours together in varying degrees helps achieve the dark, starry, deep blue winter's sky that you are aiming for once the cake has baked. Divide the mixture between the tins and bake for 20 minutes or until a skewer inserted in the centre of the cakes comes out clean. Leave in the tins to cool for 5 minutes before turning out on to wire racks to cool completely.

4. While the cakes are baking, line a shallow baking tray with baking parchment. Crush the mints by placing them in a freezer bag and bashing them into crumbs using a rolling pin. Place the crushed mint pieces on the tray, not too far apart. Put this tray into the oven when you take the cakes out and leave for 5–10 minutes, until the mints melt together into a big thin sheet of sugar glass, then immediately remove from the oven. Keep a close eye on them so that they don't burn. While the mint is still molten, sprinkle blue glitter over it and leave to set completely.

5. To make the frosting, beat the cream cheese and icing sugar together. Spread a very thin layer of frosting over each cake – a 'crumb coat'. Set aside for 20–30 minutes in the fridge to firm up, then sandwich the cakes together with frosting and liberally spread the rest over the whole cake.

6. Just before serving, break the glittery sugar glass into shards and stick into the cake. Sprinkle with glitter, if desired.

Las Posadas are an important Mexican Christmas tradition. 'Posada' means 'inn' or 'lodging' and the nine-day fiesta leading up to Christmas Day revolves around re-enactments of Mary and Joseph's journey to Bethlehem and their search for shelter. The celebrations begin with a procession and end with the sharing of food and drink, and – for children especially – the breaking of a papier mâché piñata filled with sweets and gifts. This piñata-style cake is a great way to share in the celebrations. Sally filled her chocolate-flavoured cake with Smarties for a colourful surprise when the cake is sliced, but you can use any chocolates or sweets you like. It's a cake that's bound to get people talking as the admiring recipients try to work out how on earth you got the treats inside.

Sally Biggs

PIÑATA CAKE

SERVES 16–20

340g unsalted butter, softened

340g caster sugar

225g self-raising flour

115g cocoa powder

6 medium eggs

splash of milk

FILLING AND FROSTING

900ml double cream

118g strawberry flavour Angel Delight (or choose your favourite flavour)

250g sugar-coated chocolates, such as Smarties, M&M's etc.

multi-coloured sprinkles, to decorate

sliced strawberries, to decorate (optional)

1. Preheat the oven to 180°C/fan 160°C/gas 4. Grease and line four 20cm sandwich tins.

2. Beat the butter and sugar using a wooden spoon or electric mixer, until light and fluffy. Sift the flour and cocoa powder together into a separate bowl.

3. Add one egg and a tablespoon of the flour mixture to the butter and beat briefly until combined. Keep repeating this step until all the eggs, flour and cocoa have been added. Add the splash of milk with the final addition of flour and cocoa and fold until thoroughly combined.

4. Divide the mixture between the tins. Bake for 20–25 minutes, until the tops spring back when lightly pressed and a skewer inserted in the centre of the cakes comes out clean. Leave to cool in the tins for 5–10 minutes before turning out on to wire racks to cool completely.

5. When cool, cut a 15cm round hole in the centre of two of the cakes.

6. To make the filling and frosting, beat the double cream and Angel Delight with an electric whisk, until it has a spreadable consistency.

7. To assemble, spread a layer of frosting over one of the whole sponges then top with one of the sponges with the hole. Spread more frosting around the ring of sponge and place the other sponge with the hole on top of that and spread more frosting over it. Pour the sugar-coated chocolates into the hole. Finally top with the last whole sponge. Spread the remaining frosting over the top and down the sides of the cake. Decorate the top with the sprinkles and strawberries (if using). This cake is best stored in the fridge and eaten within 3 days.

Lynn Hill
Founder of
Clandestine Cake Club

Every year, the British Met Office makes predictions about the chances of the UK enjoying a white Christmas, and every year they seem to get lower and lower. As children press their noses to the windows in search of those elusive flakes, you can be sure to enjoy a white Christmas Eve at home by baking this wintery-white snowflake cake. Let it snow stars of vanilla buttercream and crisp sugary meringues, and don't forget to leave a slice out for Santa. (Pictured overleaf.)

VANILLA SNOWFLAKE CAKE

SERVES 10–12

225g unsalted butter, softened

225g caster sugar (or vanilla caster sugar if you have it)

4 medium eggs, lightly beaten

225g self-raising flour, sifted

1½ tsp vanilla paste

1 tbsp milk (optional)

2 tbsp raspberry preserve

MERINGUES

3 medium egg whites

180g caster sugar

1. Make the meringues, ideally the day before or ahead. This mixture will make around 100 star/snowflake shapes using a star nozzle. Around 50–55 are needed to decorate the cake.

2. Preheat the oven to 120°C/fan 100°C/gas ½. Line a baking tray with baking parchment.

3. In a spotlessly clean bowl, whisk the egg whites using an electric whisk until soft peaks form. Gradually add the sugar and continue whisking until the meringue is nice and shiny. Rub a little meringue between your thumb and finger; if there is no graininess, your meringue is ready. Transfer the meringue to a large piping bag fitted with a star nozzle. To stop the parchment from moving around on the baking tray, pipe a little meringue on to the baking tray and stick the parchment to it, then pipe as many star shapes of about 2cm wide as you can on to the baking parchment. Pipe a couple of slightly larger stars for the central decoration.

4. Bake in the oven for 30 minutes or until the meringues are crisp and dry. Turn off the heat and leave the door open until they cool completely. Keep in a container until you are ready to decorate your cake.

5. Increase the oven setting to 200°C/fan 180°C/gas 6. Grease and line two 20cm sandwich tins.

6. Beat the butter and sugar using a wooden spoon or electric whisk, until light and fluffy. Add the eggs one at a time, beating well after each addition, and adding a tablespoon of flour with the final egg to prevent curdling. Add the vanilla paste and mix until well combined. Gently fold in the remaining flour until combined. If the mixture looks a little stiff, add a tablespoon or so of milk to loosen it and reach a dropping consistency. Divide the mixture evenly between the tins.

7. Bake for 20–25 minutes or until a skewer inserted in the centre of the cakes comes out clean. Remove from the oven and allow to cool in the tins for 5–10 minutes, then turn out on to a wire rack to cool completely.

WHITE CHOCOLATE SWISS MERINGUE BUTTERCREAM

150g white chocolate, broken into pieces

4 medium egg whites

220g caster sugar

360g unsalted butter, softened, cut into 1cm cubes

1½ tsp vanilla paste

8. Make the Swiss meringue buttercream. Place the chocolate in a bowl set over a pan of simmering water. Allow to melt, then take off the heat, give it a stir and leave to one side to cool a little.

9. Place the egg whites and sugar into a large clean bowl set over a pan of simmering water. Using a electric hand whisk, whisk until the meringue is silky smooth and not grainy. The temperature must reach 88°C to cook the egg whites. This will take 8–10 minutes. Remove the bowl from the heat and continue to whisk the meringue until it thickens and cools to room temperature.

10. Add the butter in small batches – about 2–3 cubes at a time – beating well after each addition. It may slacken a little to begin with, but keep mixing until all the butter is added. Add the vanilla and mix until well combined.

11. Use a whisk to beat in the cooled melted chocolate until well combined. Leave to one side until you are ready to cover your cake.

12. To assemble, level both cakes with a serrated knife to ensure all surfaces are flat. Place one of the cakes on a cake stand and spread the raspberry preserve over the top, then sandwich the two layers together.

13. Cover the whole cake with a very thin layer of buttercream – a 'crumb coat', and set aside for 20–30 minutes in the fridge. Now cover the whole cake with buttercream, smoothing down the top and sides. Fill a large piping bag fitted with a star nozzle with the remainder. Decorate the sides of the cake first, alternating rows of piped buttercream stars with the small snowflake meringues. Now do the same on top, finishing off with one of the larger star-shaped meringues in the centre. Sandwich together any leftover snowflakes with any remaining buttercream for an afternoon tea treat the next day.

Everyone has their own favourite traditions for Christmas Day and the cake to enjoy over the festive period is often a cause for debate. Hopefully you will find your festive cake joy somewhere in this book, whether your preference is for a chocolate Yule log (see page 194), a traditional fruit cake, or as in many households, a sumptuous fruit stollen like this handsome specimen. Heidi's version is a little lighter than many typical recipes as it doesn't have the hefty marzipan and she's added quark (low-fat curd cheese), a traditional ingredient in German baking, which adds moisture while keeping the cake's texture light. It's packed with all the traditional festive flavours: walnuts, cranberries, booze and spice. Merry Christmas!

Heidi Fulton-Cummins

WALNUT AND CRANBERRY STOLLEN

SERVES 12–15

500g plain flour

1 tbsp baking powder

150g caster sugar

pinch of salt

1 tsp ground cinnamon

1 tsp vanilla essence

1 tsp rum essence

1 tsp almond essence

2 medium eggs

175g butter, cold

250g lemon-flavoured or plain quark

grated zest of 1 unwaxed lemon

100g dried cranberries

100g ground walnuts

100g walnuts, roughly chopped

DECORATION

50g unsalted butter, melted

50g icing sugar

1 tsp ground cinnamon

10 walnut halves

1. Preheat the oven to 180°C/fan 160°C/gas 4. Grease and line a large baking tray with a lip.

2. Sift the flour and baking powder into a large bowl and make a well in the middle. Add the sugar, salt, cinnamon, all of the essences and the eggs. Mix part of the flour from the side of the well in with these ingredients to create a thick mixture. Grate the butter over this and loosely mix with a metal spoon. Add the remaining ingredients and mix with the spoon, then bring together with your hands. The mixture will be quite stiff.

3. Transfer to a lightly floured work surface and form into a traditional oval stollen shape, about 30cm long.

4. Place on the baking tray and bake for 1¼–1½ hours, until a skewer inserted in the centre comes out clean. Turn twice during baking so that it colours evenly. Remove from the oven and immediately brush all over with the melted butter, then leave to cool.

5. When cool, mix the icing sugar and cinnamon and dredge over the stollen, then cover with the walnuts. It's ideal to leave the cake for at least 1 day before slicing and eating it. This allows the flavours to develop and gives the melted butter a chance to penetrate the firm crust on the cake, producing a more even texture. Do wrap it in baking parchment and foil.

While some would argue that Boxing Day was simply an excuse for the British to enjoy an extra day of holiday, others claim its origins date from the nineteenth century as the day when servants and tradespeople were each given a gift by their employer known as a Christmas box. Either way, it remains a public holiday in the UK and is traditionally spent with family and friends. So, why not make your own box of deliciousness to offer to loved one? Sitting on a base of crunchy crumbled meringue is a fruity, frozen cream infused with all the flavours of Christmas – including some mince pie filling. It's a lifesaver of a cake at this time of year as it can be prepared well in advance.

Laure Moyle

FROZEN BOX OF DELICIOUSNESS

SERVES 12–16

6 all-butter mince pies

100g candied peel

2 generous tbsp Armagnac

2 tsp ground cinnamon

1 tsp ground ginger

pinch of ground nutmeg

grated zest of 1 orange

300ml double cream

150g ricotta cheese

6 meringue nests, crumbled

100g flaked almonds

DECORATION (OPTIONAL)

1 x packet ready-to-roll sugarpaste, in the colour of your choice

icing sugar, to dust

1. Grease and line the base and sides of an 18cm loose-bottomed square cake tin, allowing an extra 2.5cm of paper above the rim for easy removal.

2. Lift off the mince pie lids, scoop the filling into a small saucepan, and roughly crumble the pastry shells into a separate bowl for later.

3. Add the candied peel, Armagnac, spices and orange zest to the saucepan. Bring to a gentle boil, then take off the heat and leave to cool. You should have a jam consistency.

4. In another bowl, whip the cream to soft peaks. Fold in the cool candied fruit mix, add the ricotta, folding gently until just combined (don't overmix the filling or it will lose its lightness), then fold in the crumbled meringue.

5. Spoon enough cream mixture into the tin so that it comes halfway up the sides. Be sure to spread it all the way into the corners, but without moving the meringue pieces around too much.

6. Sprinkle the crumbled mince pie pastry over the top, then cover with more cream mixture up to the rim of the tin. Level it and scatter with the almonds. Place in the freezer overnight or until needed.

7. When you're ready to serve, remove the tin from the freezer and run a blowtorch (or your hands!) along the sides of the tin. Use the extra paper edge to lift the cake out of the tin and place on a serving plate.

8. If you'd like to decorate with a bow, roll out the sugarpaste on a work surface lightly dusted with icing sugar, until 3–4mm thick. Cut into a long strip, or strips, and shape into a bow. Alternatively, decorate with chocolate bows or any other decorations you like.

The first edition of *Children's and Household Tales* (later known as *Grimm's Fairy Tales*), written by brothers Jacob and Wilhelm Grimm, was first published in Germany in December 1812. Stories have been added to the collection over the years and it now includes over 200 folkloric tales. When the book was first published, German bakers were inspired by the story of Hansel and Gretel, the two children imprisoned by a wicked witch in her edible gingerbread house, to create decorative biscuit houses of their own. The tradition has endured and baking or buying a gingerbread house is now a common Christmas ritual in Germany and beyond. Bake and decorate these gingerbread biscuits, stack them around a beautifully light spiced fruit cake, and continue the tradition for yourself, with the added bonus of a slice of cake to enjoy for your efforts.

Carla Scott

GINGERBREAD VILLAGE CAKE

SERVES 16–18

250g Stork margarine or unsalted butter, softened

100g caster sugar

125g soft light brown sugar

4 large eggs

225g self-raising flour

1 tsp baking powder

1 tsp mixed spice

100g ground almonds

500g mixed dried fruit (containing mixed peel)

GINGERBREAD

100g unsalted butter

100g soft light brown sugar

100g golden syrup

225g plain flour

1 tsp bicarbonate of soda

1 tsp ground ginger

❯ *Ingredients and recipe continue overleaf*

1. Preheat the oven to 170°C/fan 150°C/gas 3. Grease and line a 23cm springform cake tin.

2. Beat the margarine, sugars and eggs using an electric whisk or the paddle attachment in a stand mixer.

3. Sift the flour, baking powder and mixed spice into another bowl. Add the ground almonds, mix thoroughly and then add to the margarine mixture and beat again until smooth. Fold in the mixed dried fruit. Tip into the tin and smooth the top. Line the outside of the tin with brown paper and put a piece of baking parchment on top.

4. Place in the oven on the middle shelf and bake for 1½–1¾ hours until firm to the touch and a skewer inserted in the centre of the cake comes out clean. Leave in the tin for 20 minutes and then turn out on to a wire rack to cool completely.

5. To make the gingerbread houses, have ready two baking trays (approximately 30 x 30cm) and two large squares of baking parchment. Lightly oil the parchment.

6. Put the butter, sugar and golden syrup into a pan and heat until just melted – it doesn't need to bubble.

7. Sift the flour, bicarbonate of soda and ginger together then add them to the pan and beat until everything comes together. Divide the mixture in half and place in the middle of each piece of parchment tray. Shape the mixture into a square and then gently roll out until it's the thickness of a pound coin. You can use a plastic ruler to keep shaping it into a square, it's a very forgiving mixture to work with. You should end up with two pieces about 23 x 23cm. Carefully transfer the baking parchment to the baking trays. ❯

ICING FOR HOUSES

240g icing sugar,
plus extra to dust

2 tbsp water

ICING FOR CAKE

350g icing sugar

50ml water

8. Bake one sheet at a time so you can cut the first while the next one bakes. Place on the middle shelf and bake for 15 minutes – it will still be soft but golden and perhaps very slightly overcooked at the edges. Remove from the oven and put the other tray in.

9. Trim a tiny bit off the edges of the square to neaten it up while it's still hot. Then you need to cut out the house. Use a ruler, a long cook's knife and a smaller knife with no serrated edge. You need to work quite quickly before it cools and becomes brittle to cut. Cut rectangles 4cm x 10–12cm; as you can see in the picture, the houses are various heights. Altogether you need 18 houses – there will be leftovers, but they won't last long. Once you have cut the basic rectangles you need to cut out the roofs so cut off little triangles, again at different heights to make the overall effect more interesting. Repeat with the second tray of gingerbread, then leave to cool completely.

10. To ice the houses, mix the icing sugar and water – it needs to be of piping consistency so you may find you need to add a little more sugar or water. Put in a piping bag fitted with a 4mm plain nozzle. Line up all the houses and decorate the backs first. Only pipe decoration on to the top half as the rest is stuck on the cake. Leave these to dry – it only takes a few minutes. Carefully turn the houses over and pipe decoration on to the fronts – doors, windows and snowy rooflines, depending on your preference. Leave to dry.

11. Once the cake is completely cool, make up the cake icing by mixing the icing sugar and water – it needs to coat the back of a spoon thickly. Using a quarter of the icing, spread a very thin layer all around the side of the cake then put the rest on the top, keeping back about 2 tablespoons to use as 'glue' for the houses and gently spread this to the edge of the cake.

12. One at a time, spread a little icing on the back of each house and stick it to the cake, door facing outwards and leaving 3–5mm of space between each house to allow room for a knife to cut slices. Once all the houses are on, dust the roof tops and top of the cake with icing sugar to finish the scene.

A Dundee is a type of fruit cake, traditionally soaked in a good glug of whisky and infused with Scottish marmalade. It is distinguishable from other fruit cakes on account of its iconic decoration: concentric rings of whole blanched almonds. To celebrate Hogmanay, the Scottish term for the last day of the year, there is no cake more fitting. This light, crumbly version breaks from tradition – the fruit is soaked in brandy for a mellower, warming note; zingy orange zest replaces the sweeter marmalade, and the almonds have been exchanged for Brazil nuts to give the top a richer flavour. Despite the twists, it's perfect with a wee dram, so serve yourself a whopping slice as you count down to midnight and bring in the New Year.

Lynn Hill
Founder of
Clandestine Cake Club

DUNDEE CAKE

SERVES 8–10

225g currants

225g raisins

225g sultanas

50ml brandy or sherry

300g self-raising flour

2 tsp mixed spice

1 tsp nutmeg

pinch of salt

100g glacé cherries, rinsed and patted dry, quartered

grated zest of 1 large lemon

grated zest of 1 large orange, plus the juice of ½

225g unsalted butter, softened

225g soft light brown sugar

5 medium eggs, lightly beaten

25–30 whole Brazil nuts

1. Mix the currants, raisins and sultanas together in a bowl. Add the brandy and give it another good mix. Leave in the bowl overnight for the fruit to soak up the brandy or for at least 6 hours.

2. Preheat the oven to 160°C/fan 140°C/gas 3. Grease and line a 20cm deep-sided, loose-bottomed cake tin with baking parchment, leaving an extra 5cm above the rim of the tin. Wrap the outside of the tin with brown paper and secure it with kitchen string – this helps prevent the edges overbaking.

3. Sift the flour, spices and salt together and leave to one side. Add the chopped cherries to the mixed fruit and stir. Add both zests and the orange juice and stir well to ensure all the juice and zest are evenly distributed around the dried fruit.

4. In a separate bowl, beat the butter and sugar using a wooden spoon or electric whisk until light and fluffy. Add the eggs one at a time, beating well after each addition, and adding a tablespoon of the flour mixture with each egg to prevent curdling. Fold in the remaining flour mixture and stir until well combined.

5. Add all the fruit and mix well until evenly distributed. Pour into the cake tin and decorate the top of the cake with the Brazil nuts. Bake for 2¼–2½ hours or until a skewer inserted in the centre of the cake comes out clean. After the cake has baked for 1 hour 50 minutes, cover the top with foil to prevent it browning too fast. Leave in the tin to cool completely before turning out on to a wire rack or cake plate. This cake will keep for several weeks if wrapped and kept in an airtight container.

INDEX

ACKNOWLEDGEMENTS

Once again I would like to thank all the CCC members who submitted their wonderful recipes for this book.

Many thanks to my literary agents Stuart Cooper and Claire Potter of Metrostar Media who continue to help and support me as CCC grows. Your guidance, and a shoulder to cry on at some difficult times, have been unwavering; I consider you my friends.

Thanks go to everyone at Quercus Books: particularly to Ione Walder and Imogen Fortes who made this second book an equal joy and as much fun to do as the first book.

Many thanks to Kat Mead, who tested all the recipes and made them for Kris Kirkham to take such wonderful pictures – they both brought the cakes to life with a vision of celebration. Thanks to Kris's assistant, Faith Mason, and to Pene Parker, whose design skills have made this a truly stunning celebratory book that I am proud of.

Last but not least, to my family David, Joanne and Richard, whose love and support have helped me continue with my passion for CCC and for eating all the cakes that I have made over the years, especially when it came to testing my recipes for this book.

I love you all.

Lynn Hill

CONTRIBUTORS' WEBSITES

Charlotte Pike	www.charlotteskitchendiary.com
Chintal Kakaya	www.chinskitchen.co.uk
Clare Conlon	www.aweebitofcake.blogspot.co.uk
Fiona Bevans	www.teaandtakes.com
Gemma Johnson	www.gemmathebaker.com
Jelena Culum	www.missjwonders.wordpress.com
Jen Storey	www.spiffybaking.blogspot.com
Jen Dyke	www.bakearama.wordpress.com
Laure Moyle	www.puddingfairy.co.uk
Mike Wallis	www.teaandcake.co.uk
Myfanwy Hywel	www.littlebakersblog.com
Nisha Arthey	www.limetreebakery.co.uk
Rachel McGrath	www.dollybakes.co.uk
Ruth Tebbutt	www.cupcakesisters.co.uk
Sam Smith	www.theyorkshirebakery.wordpress.com
Sharon Clarkson	www.humbugshouse.wordpress.com
Susan Jones	www.eviesgran.wordpress.com

Quercus Publishing Ltd
Carmelite House
50 Victoria Embankment
London
EC4Y 0DZ

First published in Great Britain in 2015

A catalogue record of this book is available
from the British Library
ISBN 978 1 78429 071 9

Commissioning editor: Ione Walder
Project editor: Imogen Fortes
Design and prop styling: Pene Parker
Photography: Kris Kirkham
Food styling: Kat Mead
Illustration on page 223: Alex Gilmartin
CCC logo created by Anita Mangan

Printed and bound in China
10 9 8 7 6 5 4 3 2 1